A FIGHTING CHANCE

Keep advocating for
Oklahoma's
Children!
Jane
Humphries

A FIGHTING CHANCE

Supporting

YOUNG CHILDREN
EXPERIENCING
DISRUPTIVE CHANGE

JANE HUMPHRIES, EdD,
KARI RAINS, MS

Redleaf Press®
www.redleafpress.org
800-423-8309

Published by Redleaf Press
10 Yorkton Court
St. Paul, MN 55117
www.redleafpress.org

While the examples in this book are current issues seen within early childhood environments, the names and identifying details of the children and adults have been changed to protect the privacy of individuals.

First edition 2017
Cover design by Ryan Scheife, Mayfly Design
Cover Low Polygon Triangle Pattern Background courtesy Sophon Mungmeetanawong / Shutterstock
Interior design by Ryan Scheife, Mayfly Design
Typeset in the Minion Pro and Realtime Text typefaces
Interior photos by Justin Reedy Photography and Brent Niles—BBJN Designs
Printed in the United States of America
24 23 22 21 20 19 18 17   1 2 3 4 5 6 7 8

CIP data is on file with the Library of Congress

Printed on acid-free paper

*In remembrance of those children who died, those who survived,
and those changed forever on April 19, 1995.*

*Because of this tragedy, we continually work in research and expand our knowledge in the
areas of trauma and resiliency, which impact the lives of children daily.*

*As we add to the growing collection of resources, we celebrate those in the field of early
childhood who are committed to supporting children who experience disruptive change.*

Contents

Foreword

Welcome.

I am glad you are here to join me in reading this informative, quietly powerful and hopeful book by Jane Humphries and Kari Rains. *A Fighting Chance: Supporting Young Children Experiencing Disruptive Change* is one of those books that goes beyond being words on pages to engaging readers in a conversation that invites each of us working on behalf of young children and their families to see that we can make a difference.

The book is grounded in the personal and professional experiences and insights of the authors. Jane Humphries was director and a parent in a child care program six blocks north of the scene of the Oklahoma City bombing, what one of the children described as a "volcano," on April 19, 1995. This deadliest act of domestic terrorism in the United States led the field of early childhood education to begin to understand the impact of traumatic events on children. Kari Rains brings her perspective of working one-on-one in early intervention with children experiencing the disruption of medical, emotional, and stressed home environments.

Jane and Kari's collective deep understanding of the challenges posed by disruptive change, their knowledge and skill of trauma and resilience, and their confidence and clarity are affirmed on page 2 when Jane, who had been off-site consulting, tells of racing back to her son and her program—at over a hundred miles per hour—the morning of the Oklahoma City bombing: "All I could think of was getting everyone indoors, secure in their classrooms, and engaged in daily activity—something normal—to help all of us move forward."

They offer us a rich blend of research findings, concrete recommendations, and strategies to highlight and use intentionally in daily interactions with children. Foremost, this book is a call for each of us to commit to being an ongoing learner—about children, about trauma and resilience, and perhaps most important of all, about ourselves. Why? Because in the parlance of Jane and Kari, teachers are a bridge of hope for young children and their families.

For those of us who support teachers—whether as leaders, coaches, mentors, consultants, or writers—this image underscores the importance of our efforts to work in partnership with our colleagues, teachers whose daily interactions and decisions have the potential to strengthen family relationships and literally shape children's brains and life paths.

Instances of acute and complex trauma have become more of the norm for many children. In response, many of us find ourselves reeling with our emotions, those of children and families and the harsh truth that traumatic events can have an impact on all areas of development, beginning in infancy and continuing throughout a child's lifetime.

Giving a child a fighting chance is demanding work. As Jane and Kari describe, it can be "intense, tedious, frustrating, challenging, and stressful." Yet at the same time, teachers' relationships and daily interactions with children and families have the potential to change the future trajectory of the lives of a child and family.

Jane, for example, tells about how years later she reconnected with a young woman who had been a child when Jane was a classroom teacher. Megan (not her real name), who had experienced disruptive change, now a student in one of Jane's online college courses, shared with Jane her fond memories of interactions and how the classroom in Jane's program "felt like a home." Megan's mother, years later, thanked Jane and her staff for hanging in there with Megan and attributed her success today to their nurturing.

Megan's story is a reminder, I suggest, for each of us to ask ourselves, "What do I hope a child and family will say about their early education experience in twenty years?"

The authors have chosen to use executive function as a framework of intervention that fosters and supports resiliency, because executive function skills help children manage thoughts, actions, and emotions to achieve goals (Miyake et al. 2000), and they can be improved (Diamond and Lee 2011).

The main body of the book is a series of case stories, many from Kari's practice. Here we meet children, including Gracie and Quinton, experiencing homelessness and parental incarceration. We meet twins Taylor and Tate who faced major disruptions in their care by their primary family adults; two-year-old Jasmine whose mother was killed in a convenience store robbery; and Noah whose father died suddenly and unexpectedly. We find stories about children who have experienced the impact of a natural disaster, who have lived within a state's foster care system, and who are facing the disruption of a medical diagnosis.

For each story and child, hands-on, doable strategies are identified that teachers, whether in centers or family child care homes, can use to promote the seven essential life skills identified by Ellen Galinsky (2010, 4) in her book, *Mind in the Making*:

- focus and self-control

- perspective taking

- communicating

- making connections

- critical thinking

- taking on challenges

- self-directed, engaged learning

As many of us know, there is no secret recipe to giving children a fighting chance, no expensive equipment to be bought. It would be easier if there were such a solution. Rather, the authors lead us to look with deeper clarity and appreciation at foundational elements of quality practice that we all know so well, including:

- everyday interactions and activities

- rituals and routines

- communication between adults

- impact of touch and voice

- classroom arrangement and management

- observing, noting, and responding to children's individual differences

These seemingly basic strategies make me realize how easy it is to take for granted how vitally important it is that we shine a light on the critical role teachers and EI specialists play in their daily interactions with children and families. Here are just a few examples:

- *the writing of postcards* to provide Quentin with a safe way to communicate with his incarcerated parents

- *reassurance* to Quentin that his father was being fed and had a blanket at night just like he did at child care and at his grandparents' home

- *providing a sense of control* over her life disrupted by the death of her mother by letting Jasmine lead the other children to the playground and make choices about lunch, free play, and outside play

- *validating fears* to help Amal who experienced a tornado feel more in control

- *arranging seating and providing a weighted lap pillow* to help Alice be able to experience lunch with her classmates without taking their food, a common behavior of children experiencing the complex trauma that is often associated with being in foster care

A Fighting Chance ends where it begins: with a focus on you and me and on our colleagues; on our work as individuals and as collaborative team members working on behalf of a child and family.

Jane and Kari remind us that "the key to being successful is learning and understanding the perspective of what is taking place in the child's life and then adjusting *yourself and the approach to respond to the child* accordingly." Or in the words of a dear friend and colleague, Jeree Pawl: "How you are is as important as what you say and do." And if I might, as my friends and colleagues Judy Jablon and Charlotte Stetson and I wrote in *Powerful Interactions: How to Connect with Children to Extend Their Learning*, "Giving your interactions some careful thinking is important because research shows that who you are, and how and what you say and do as you engage with children, makes a difference in what they learn about themselves, others, and the world."

Over forty years ago, when I was heading the Bank Street Infant and Family Center, my adviser, Dorothy Gross, said to me, "You are your own best resource." These five words have stayed with me always and have shaped my sense of self as a professional and my teaching and writing with and for colleagues ever since. You are your own best resource too. *A Fighting Chance* will help each of us appreciate and build on our strengths as we extend our learning together on behalf of children and families—today and into the future.

—Amy Laura Dombro

Acknowledgments

We first want to extend our gratitude to Roger and Bonnie Neugebauer as well as Donna Rafanello with *Child Care Exchange* for working with us as the written ideas became published articles that ultimately lead to the creation of this book. It was their commitment to working with and publishing our work that captured the attention of Kara Lomen and Laurie Herrmann at Redleaf Press. This adventure in writing also provided us the opportunity to work with Heidi Hogg who, through her editorial skills, provided additional insight and crafting as this book evolved. From the work of numerous researchers and authors, we were able to include insights from the work of Ellen Galinsky, Dr. Paula Jorde Bloom, Margie Carter, and Deb Curtis to assist our work. All are "giants" in our field who have contributed greatly to the continued understanding of child development and the continued professional development of those who work with children and families each day. We also wish to thank Amy Laura Dombro for contributing a foreword to our book and eloquently connecting understanding of our direction and intent to the early childhood community.

The stories in this book have come to life out of our collective years of work with children and their families along with the work of many of our dedicated early childhood professional colleagues. Through these experiences, those working in the classroom and program environments were connected with the many necessary professionals in their communities providing mental health, social work, and child development services, and medical supports such as pediatricians, physical and occupational therapists, and speech-language pathologists. All of these worked in tandem to support children and families rocked by disruptive change. The common thread among all of these professionals who were working together was their commitment and willingness to stand alongside and intervene as the disruptive change event evolved. They never quit believing, nor did they stop working alongside the early childhood program staff. Thank you to the many women and men who worked with Dr. Jane beginning at St. Luke's Children's Center many years ago while teaming with Dr. Laurna Champ who provided on-site mental health consultation and services to assist the staff and families. As the years continued, Dr. Jane and Kari were fortunate to work with many gifted early intervention team members that support Oklahoma's intervention programs. We also wish to thank specific individuals and organizations whose many experiences and talents were shared to support this effort: Kristy Willingham, Michelle Campbell-Gaylord, Nancy Potter, Justin Reedy, Brent Niles, Beckie Osborn, Iowa Tribe of Oklahoma Early Head Start, Stillwater Early Head Start, Perkins-Tryon Elementary School, and the Oklahoma City National Memorial and Museum.

Last, but by no means least, we are grateful for the support of our families. Both of us had parents who provided us childhoods in which we were loved dearly and afforded opportunities to become highly educated. We both met and married two wonderful guys, Mike and Darrick, who have respected and supported our independent spirits and need to write and be creative. And, most importantly, they partnered with us to be committed parents to our children. Michael, Ella, Nick, and Nate—we are proud to be your moms, and it is through you that we have experienced and been able to share with others our greatest lessons and growth within our field of child development.

Introduction

I t was a beautiful spring morning. Chilly, but the sun was shining and the flowers were blooming. I had some consulting work about eleven miles outside of the Oklahoma City area. My mom dropped by my house to pick up my two-year-old son, and off they went to downtown Oklahoma City. He went to the child care facility where I, Jane Humphries, was director, and my mom went to her office job at the Episcopal Diocese. I arrived at the location where I was consulting to meet a colleague of mine. Our morning began at the Head Start program. Children were coming and going, their parents waving good-bye and chatting with teachers. It was just before 9:00 a.m., and the teachers were finishing breakfast and transitioning to circle time. Just another day, so we thought. But then at 9:01 a.m., an event took place—the deadliest act of domestic terrorism in the United States, which took the lives of more than 150 adults. Even more stunning, the lives of children—infants, toddlers, preschoolers—and their teachers and the director of the child care program inside the building were lost. This was the first major event that riveted an entire nation within minutes, and yet it also was the catalyst for the field of early childhood education to begin understanding the impact of traumatic events on children.

Of course I didn't know any of that at the time. Within minutes, I was racing toward my son, toward the child care facility where I was director, toward the dark smoke—me and two Oklahoma Highway Patrol cars. I knew it was bad when I was going ninety to one hundred miles per hour and the officers flew past me and never gave me a blink. I slid in behind them, and within minutes I was at my program. The teachers and children were all standing out on the playground, staring at the plume of dark smoke that was directly six blocks south of our location. As I jumped out of the car, the children started pointing and yelling, "Look, Ms. Jane! It's a volcano!" The teachers were speechless. As I gazed around, all I could think of was getting everyone indoors, secure in their classrooms, and engaged in daily activity—something normal—to help *all* of us move forward. I also needed to find out what the heck was going on! As the staff looked to me, I said, "Let's get in our classrooms and get an activity started. Shut your classroom doors, and let's avoid having upset parents coming in to get their children—we're going to get through this day." I immediately grabbed a TV and dragged it into my office. Just enough time had gone by that officials had determined it was far worse than some sort of explosion tied to a gas leak.

The media started reporting that this was a terrorist attack—a bombing. No one knew who or what was responsible. Outwardly scared and concerned parents began hurrying into the facility. We immediately stopped them in the hallways because we did not know exactly which parents were coming for their children and which were not (many of the parents worked in the downtown area). I had enough wits about me to know that the children in the classroom did not need to see parents who were obviously emotional. When those first parents arrived, we could clearly see the panic on their faces (which was understandable, of course). The last thing I wanted was for our children to be further traumatized by whatever this horrific event was.

As the day wore on, our horror grew, and the reality started sinking in for me, my staff, the children, and their families—we were victims of the largest act of domestic terrorism in the United States. The days, months, and years since have had a lasting impact and left footprints on all of us for the rest of our lives. As the world watched, Oklahoma became the model for research on the impact of trauma, for learning how to heal, for heeding lessons learned, and for giving—sometimes to perfect strangers—whatever was needed: what the world now knows as the "Oklahoma Standard." We became the observed lessons of resilience.

From a program perspective, my idea of a "safe" area to work—meaning early childhood, with its "typical" disruptions—had been changed for forever. While the days and years have rolled by, so many other events have taken place. Sadly, six years after the Oklahoma City bombing, airplanes were purposefully flown into the World Trade Center towers in New York. When I picked him up from school, my child—eight years old at the time—said to me in a panicked tone, with wide eyes, "You know, Mom, it was like that day when there was all that black smoke and loud noises." A major disruptive event that took place when he was two years old, innocently playing out on the playground, had left memories that I, as a parent and early childhood professional, would *never* be able to erase.

Over time, I have learned what I *can* do: constantly learn and create environments that have consistency and security. I have also recognized the power of working with a dynamic and committed teaching staff who surround me and the children with an incredible love for the work they do each day. They are what my son and many, many other children who have had traumatic experiences in their lives needed to cope and function with others in an early childhood program environment as well as within their home environments.

Kari, on the other hand, has observed trauma from a one-on-one perspective. Years of early intervention work, either in homes or in clinic environments, have allowed her to see the disruption of medical and emotional trauma as well as the stressed home environments that surround these children. While treating these families with tremendous respect and acknowledging they are the experts on their children, Kari has helped adult family members confront their own issues and poor choices, and has educated family members about better parenting options and care for their children. This work has also extended into early childhood environments, where programs try to balance the needs of typically developing children with those who require extra care and attention. Many of these programs, underresourced and underfunded, have staffs with hearts of gold and a willingness to do what they can for the children in their care. Practicality has had to become the leading strategy when working with these programs.

Our experiences as educators have ranged from daily work life to extreme events. Many early childhood professionals are dealing each day with disruptive change in the lives of the young children enrolled in their programs. These disruptions can impede a child's emotional competence, which often results in stress for those working in the program environment. With a plethora of research readily accessible that provides information on brain development, the field of early childhood has started to focus on executive function, social-emotional regulation, and the impact of trauma and toxic stress in children's lives, mixed with a multitude of disorder diagnoses. All are areas that can be overwhelming to think about—much less do something about. This leaves the adults working in the early childhood environment grappling with these questions:

- Where do we start when dealing with a child who struggles within the daily classroom environment?

- How can the adults who are tasked with being one of the few consistencies in this child's life hang on and embrace these children as they face disruptive change in their lives?

- How do we see beyond the tantrums, meltdowns, hurting of others, and self-harm, as well as other disruptions throughout the classroom day?

- How can we continue to have communication with the many adults who enter into or exit from the child's life?

Children today are living and learning to function in many societal circumstances, some more complicated than others. We as early childhood professionals can either remain stunned by this changing landscape of society and ignore the impact on young children and their families, or we can seek out information, resources, and activities that support the children in their classrooms. As authors, our hope is that this book will lend practical solutions and approaches to give the children in your care a fighting chance—not only in the classroom or program environment but also in daily life. Early childhood professionals can change the trajectory of these children's lives, and the many key elements discussed throughout this book will help you learn how to do just that.

Thank you for seeking out more information, being willing to try new and multiple things, and believing in these children. This work is hard work, and frankly, not everyone can do it. From the global administrative visions to one-on-one interactions, we hope to provide you with insights and practical solutions, as well as remind you of how important it will be to provide flexibility and consistency in your approach with *all* of the children who are a part of your daily work.

Enjoy learning more!
Dr. Jane and Kari

CHAPTER 1

Becoming the Bridge of Hope

Understanding Children's Behavior When Change Is Wreaking Havoc in Their Lives

Societal events that cause disruptive change, such as incarceration of a parent, substance abuse, parent abandonment, and varying mental health issues, have unfortunately become disturbing trends in the lives of young children. In addition to societal trends, human-made or natural disasters also impact children and may result in challenging behaviors. As those working with young children, we know we need to address these behaviors daily, if not hourly, to support children's healthy neurological and overall development. Within these chapters, you'll find many practical ideas and strategies for answering the challenges young children face daily. The foundation for these strategies includes the following elements:

- communication among the significant adults in the child's life

- consistent nurturing responses to behaviors within the classroom with carefully planned activities

- commitment to provide each child who is struggling with an informed, coordinated, calm, and nurturing environment

- ongoing access to information and resources to increase personal knowledge and understanding

Creating opportunities for resilience hinges on early childhood providers' understanding of their pivotal role in the positive outcome for children and their families during a disruptive change event. Here's what we hope those working with young children can look forward to achieving with help from this book:

- remaining informed to better support and enhance their caregiving abilities

- implementing ideas to help children establish positive relationships

- embracing recommendations to help feel more in control and to better help the children in their care

- discovering home-to-program activities to recommend to parents or other caregivers to assist their children

- becoming empowered with new skills that strengthen the relationships that adults working in early care environments have with young children and their families

We created our book for early childhood professionals who are *willing to embrace* disruptive change in the lives of young children. Our hope is that early childhood professionals will take our suggested activities and ideas to create a stable environment for children experiencing disruptive change. In this book, you'll find immediate application of strategies as well as resources located at the back of the book to use when issues arise as you care for young children and its families. To start this journey, we've included a brief review of what studies have shown us regarding child trauma; attachment and bonding; toxic stress and its impacts on the family; brain development and the resulting impact of trauma on the child's developing executive function; and supports to foster resilience. By better understanding what research has found, teachers and caregivers can better understand and recognize the context from which these children are reacting and become a bridge of hope.

Understanding Acute and Complex Trauma

One of the key areas of working with children going through a disruptive change is a better understanding of trauma and its impact on the child. Traumas are events with resulting experiences that expose children to natural and human-made disasters. These types of events include war and terrorism, accidents, abandonment and homelessness, significant medical illness or bodily injuries, forced separation from a significant adult, community violence, media and domestic violence, child abuse, and neglect.

Strong early childhood programs are the crucial connection to relationships and the key to giving children exposed to these events a fighting chance. These environments nurture hope and strength not only for the children but for their parents or significant caregivers. To successfully strengthen the chances of a positive outcome, however, a level of understanding and commitment to these children and families is necessary. While Kari and I both acknowledged the need for understanding and commitment during our years of education and early in our careers, what has become more and more evident is that this has *not* been easy work to do, nor have the same set of approaches or strategies worked each time for every child and his or her family. But the work, while intense, tedious, frustrating, challenging, and stressful, can also provide a sense of accomplishment and reward when supporting these children. The key to successful learning and understanding is gaining perspective. Pay attention to what events are taking place in the life of a child and then adjust yourself and your approach to respond to him or her accordingly. Expecting the child to solely adjust to you and your ways will only result in extreme frustration for both of you.

Acute Trauma

The mistaken assumption that trauma is the stress surrounding children and a family is the result of an influx of misinformation about trauma. In reality, trauma is the actual event that has taken place. In some instances, this is a one-time event for a child. Sometimes referred to as *acute trauma*, events such as a hurricane, a tornado, or what took place in Dr. Jane's child's case, the bombing in Oklahoma City, take place at a specific point in time. Natural disaster events often uproot the child and family, separating them from their location with few, if any, of their belongings. While this type of trauma can cause disruption in several ways (such as the loss of home,

belongings, friendships, and neighbors, as well as relocation to a different school or child care program), generally with time, understanding, and support, children and families can be buoyed up through this traumatic event.

Unfortunately, constant media coverage of human-made and natural disasters has caused children who have been involved directly or indirectly to be worried and fearful, as well as to wonder if such an event can take place again. But the very nature of these types of events means that they are unpredictable and, sadly, often hurt others. Parents and teachers have reported seeing the repercussions of this type of trauma manifest in children as disruption in sleep, regression in development, mood swings, change in appetite, decrease in wanting to play with friends, and for school-age children, a decline in school performance. Relentless news coverage fuels worry and fear.

Nowadays we have immediate access to information about traumatic events, and exposure to these images and stories do have an impact on children. Early childhood professionals must stay vigilant to avoid having conversations in front of children and avoid watching live coverage of the event in the care setting. Furthermore, we can remind parents about the importance of limiting children's exposure to media. While all adults are certainly dealing with their own reactions to what has taken place, children model the reactions they see. The way children process and understand the events taking place impacts their abilities to comprehend and express their feelings, which may result in temporary developmental delays. For example, a toddler may regress from drinking from a cup to a bottle again—or in the midst of potty training, revert back to diapers because of the inability to control his bathroom needs. While frustrating for the adults caring for them, these perceived "slips backward" are normal and must be supported positively to include play opportunities.

Adults have reported trauma-influenced play by children recreating the disaster event. Dr. Jane witnessed this firsthand within her own program after the Oklahoma City bombing. She and her teaching staff, along with others in early childhood programs located across Oklahoma, supported this by allowing children to construct a building with blocks and destroy it. As reported by early childhood professionals directly involved in 9/11, they too witnessed but also allowed play involving toy planes or other objects "crashing" into constructed towers. In areas that experience severe weather, such as tornadoes, rehearsing a routine for what to do can be comforting for children fearful at the first sight of graying skies and rain. What early childhood programs found to be effective lends tremendously to creating supportive environments. Purchasing many types of props to allow children to assume the role of community helpers such as firefighters, police, and ambulance workers for use in dramatic play and in the block areas was essential to supporting play. This type of play, to be discussed in future chapters, provides opportunities for children to process the trauma that took place.

Complex Trauma

But what about those children who experience more than just an event? This, unfortunately, is what many early childhood professionals are discovering today about what has affected the young children in their group and home environments: multiple trauma events.

What appears to be the latest trend over this past decade are children who have several traumatic issues that take place simultaneously—also known as *complex trauma*. Examples of complex trauma include domestic violence within the home, constantly changing significant adults (either in the home or child care program), homelessness, significant health and safety issues, multiple foster home placements within a relatively short period of time, and many other disruptions in the lives of children. These children, as a result of the complex trauma, display behaviors that can become very intense and erratic. These children also experience more severe difficulties and challenges over a longer time. Many working in early childhood programs become frustrated and stressed, because the intense needs and care children experiencing complex trauma have can become overwhelming.

Unfortunately, instances of acute and complex trauma experienced by children have become more of the norm and a phenomenon that has many of us in the early childhood field grasping for practical ideas to make it through the day—and in some instances hour by hour (NCTSN 2016). It is crucial to understand that while adults have the ability to manage and cope with the traumatic event in a more doable fashion, a child's capacities are limited because of his chronological and developmental age and stage, temperament, and inexperience when managing strong emotions. Research has repeatedly shown that traumatic events can impact all areas of development, beginning in infancy and continuing throughout a child's lifetime (Ginsburg and Jablow 2015). Lasting effects can include a negative impact on the child's ability to learn, problem solve, and communicate and interact with everyone in his world. Depending upon when this takes place, attachment and bonding can be disrupted.

Bonding and Attachment

A closer look at the importance of healthy development in young children is crucial. From birth, children build meaningful relationships—commonly called the process of bonding—that support strong feelings of love and caring between the child and significant adults. Bonding is the foundational platform to building lifelong connections and attachment.

While attachment begins at birth, it builds in stages, as initially discovered in the work of John Bowlby (1969). At first, attachment ebbs and flows because of the child's willingness to let most anyone meet his physical and emotional needs. As the child develops during the first year, that willingness begins to focus on certain caregivers:

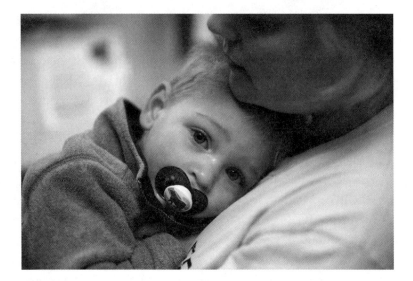

■ Primary attachments are formed mainly with the child's family members within the household and frequent caregivers.

■ Secondary attachments are formed with the child's teachers, extended family members, relatives, and neighbors. Teachers often fill this role and can serve as this attachment for several children at a time.

Both types of attachment help children experience and process the multitude of social relationships in their world that grow throughout their lifetime. Observant early childhood professionals can often begin to discern whether a child is forming secure or insecure attachments.

When evaluating secure attachment, we want to see a child who feels safe to explore and who seeks out caregivers when in unfamiliar situations and settings. A child with secure attachment can also be soothed and comforted in a manageable way. When a child is insecure, adults observe that he does *not* look to adults for comfort, reassurance, or connection. As Mary Ainsworth and her colleagues found in 1978, these behaviors are typically described in three different ways:

■ Ambivalent: The child displays behaviors that are inconsistent when seeking an attachment figure, either when responding to or attempting to connect with a caregiver.

■ Avoidant: The child is disinterested in significant adults and may even seek out strangers for comfort, rather than a primary caregiver.

- Disorganized: The child appears confused and displays behaviors when he does not particularly need or care for any adult assistance.

The overall ramifications of a child with insecure attachment can include impacts on the child's self-esteem, self-control, and neediness of adults, either in positive or negative ways. These children are often described as angry or aggressive, harmful to themselves and others, and capable of destroying objects in their environment.

Since we work with young children, recognizing the importance of bonding and attachment in a child's life is a major consideration and should be formed and supported consistently. When an insecure attachment is coupled with acute or complex trauma events, this can lead to a child's behaviors becoming unpredictable. Unpredictable behaviors can develop within the first few months after the trauma or much later in life. Either way, the result is stress that is toxic, and that impacts the child's overall development.

Toxic Stress and Its Impact

Stress is a reality in life, and we all have to learn how to cope with it.

The National Scientific Council on the Developing Child (2014) distinguishes three kinds of stress:

- Positive: This type of stress is a part of normal development and is characterized by brief increases of heart rate and mild elevations in hormone levels.

- Tolerable: This kind of stress occurs when the body's alert system is activated at a higher level but is time limited and buffered by supportive adults who assist the child when navigating the results of the stress.

- Toxic: This type happens when the child is subjected to prolonged episodes of stress, such as physical or emotional abuse, caregiver substance abuse or mental illness, severe neglect, or exposure to violence—without the support of an adult.

Children *need* healthy doses of stress to learn coping skills. In fact, our brains are wired to accept and tolerate levels of stress created by psychological and physical threats. The Alfred P. Murrah Federal Building bombing for Dr. Jane's son is an example of a tolerable stress event. Her son's body alert system reacted to the loud boom of the bomb as he was playing on the playground and the resulting shaking of the ground, noises, smoke, confusion displayed by the teachers, and sirens from the emergency response vehicles, as well as the many blaring office and home security systems set off by the concussion of the explosion. The minutes, hours, and days immediately after the event led to weeks and years of time that have allowed him to remember but react appropriately to other stressful events in his life. The key factors in his case are that the event was time limited, and his stress was managed by supportive adults who prevented his descent into toxic stress.

Unfortunately, episodes of toxic stress can begin even in the womb. Research studies have found that moms in abusive relationships or in unhealthy environments secrete stress hormones that bathe the baby in the stress hormone cortisol. And after the child is born, the chaotic atmosphere often continues. These circumstances trigger a baby's overreaction to typical sensory experiences. As the baby constantly overresponds, the child's body continues to release high levels of cortisol—which results in an altered brain chemistry. As Bruce Perry (2013) acknowledged in his work, violence, neglect, unreliability, and high noise levels impact a child's primary relationships and can then lead to a brain that is not ready to learn. Furthermore, chronic stress triggered by early adversity can cause long-term changes in the brain functions that manage behavior and emotions. Chronic stress creates a child who is unable to respond appropriately, which results in the erratic behaviors that are so difficult to manage in childhood and, even worse, in adulthood.

One study in particular, the Adverse Childhood Experiences (this is often referred to as ACEs) study, captured how traumatic events coupled with high levels of toxic stress have led to negative, long-lasting impacts on children in their adult years. This study, first published by Felitti et al. in 1998 in the *American Journal of Preventative Medicine*, with resulting follow-up studies to present day, lends important insight for those of us leading and teaching in early childhood programs. Of particular interest are findings from adults who reported witnessing adverse experiences as children. Examples of adverse experiences were violence; poverty; physical, emotional, or sexual abuse; and significant separation from parents resulting from events such as a sudden death, divorce, or parent incarceration. Ultimately, what this study found is that these events had a meaningful impact on the adults that these children became—individuals with significant and costly health concerns. How does this radiate back to the early childhood setting? For professionals working with children and families each day, being aware of what is taking place in the child's life and its probable later impact should empower our approach to help strengthen the family.

Leaders and teachers in early childhood programs find that it is important to recognize the tenets of protective factors supported by the Center for the Study of Social Policy (2015) that help to strengthen families:

- nurturing parental resilience, which helps families be able to bounce forward rather than backward when faced with issues

- fostering social connections within early childhood programs that establish networks between families and the community

- offering referrals to community supports that assist with finding a job, direction for assistance with social and community resources as well as resources that help to navigate these systems

- increasing knowledge of parenting and child development by hosting learning events as well as sharing information through daily notes, handouts, and e-mail updates

- providing high-quality developmentally appropriate classrooms within the program that support positive social and emotional competence of children

Awareness of these tenets as well as the ACEs study can not only help us understand parent actions and reactions, but also work as a preventative mechanism. For children who experience the intervention of an early childhood teacher or director, certain adverse experiences could be lessened or avoided altogether. When we have the knowledge and abilities to identify and refer or report to professional resources in the community, we can change the trajectory of a child's life. Can you imagine being one of the people in a child's life who may *decrease* the chance of drug use, obesity, alcoholism, and depression? And can you imagine thousands of such early childhood interventions taking place across the nation, thereby reducing the overall strain on economic and social systems in this country? That's a powerful mission early childhood professionals can be tasked with—becoming toxic stress-busters who strengthen families!

Brain Development

Research in the past decade has led to a significant focus on brain development. We know that the early years are learning years, with experiences shaping the brain's growth and the child's ability to reach his full potential. Research has determined that connections between the neurons start developing before birth (Shonkoff and Phillips 2000). These neurons have the ability to trigger electrical impulses and chemicals, resulting in hundreds of thousands of connections to other neurons or nerve cells. These connections combine to create the senses and can bring about the ability to hear sounds or taste foods. Initially, this process supports the fetal development of important life functions such as a heartbeat, and during this time, the fetus develops the ability to live outside of the mother's womb.

During the first years, a healthy child's brain develops rapidly to 90 percent by age six (Thatcher et al. 1996). The brain is building internal connections that support physical structure within it to bring about learning, memory, language, and other critical functions. This wiring starts out with connections that are tentative, but with constant stimulation they become solidified. Experiences provided through human interactions and play are key to these connections. This process takes place rapidly and is based on the stimulation the child receives, which then coincides with the growth and connections between neurons and the brain.

An environment that is free of abuse, neglect, and toxic stress is imperative to supporting a child's optimum brain size. One area in the brain in particular, the limbic system, is the central control of emotions. For those children in constant stress, this area becomes much too large and results in behaviors that are hypervigilant with resulting circuitry that becomes difficult to rewire. Because their system is on constant overload, even the slightest threat—one that would normally produce a small chemical reaction within a healthy child and a resulting appropriate reaction—makes these children want to run away or, worse, attack what is perceived as a threat. While this explanation seems straightforward and simple, these over-the-top responses are the main reason from the brain perspective that behaviors become challenging to manage. The good news is that a child's brain has more plasticity than an adult's—and this can allow for recovery and success.

Stressful experiences alter the function and architecture of the brain. And prolonged stressful experiences certainly trigger the need for a child to receive a multitude of services provided by a team of professionals working in tandem with the early childhood environment and personnel. It is important to keep in mind that brain plasticity continues throughout the child's development. Every new neural pathway that we help children create offers the ability to alter existing ones—ones that stress has created. The brain *can* adapt to new experiences, learn new information, and create new memories. And early childhood professionals are crucial to this healing process by being supportive and providing environments that help challenging children to learn and grow.

Children's Executive Function

Ellen Galinsky's book *Mind in the Making* (2010) is the culmination of years of her own research interviewing experts on children, as well as reading thousands of studies on children's development. Galinsky made a connection between children's development and the adult skills needed for the twenty-first century. More specifically, she pointed to the development of the prefrontal cortex of the brain, which houses what child development researchers refer to as the *executive functions* of the brain. These functions tie together our ability to manage what is taking place with the different areas of our brain's abilities, resulting in the prefrontal cortex weaving together our social, emotional, and intellectual capacities. While this emerges in the preschool years, it does not mature until young adulthood.

Galinsky (2010, 4) says, "Executive functions pull together our feelings and thinking so that we can reflect, analyze, plan, and evaluate," and she identifies seven essential life skills:

- focus and self-control

- perspective taking

- communicating

- making connections

- critical thinking

- taking on challenges

- self-directed, engaged learning

We must keep each one of these areas in mind when working with our most challenging children. Intervention can have a big payoff because, as noted by Diamond and Lee (2011), these skills can be improved. We as early childhood professionals must believe and want for children to learn ways to manage frustration, recognize and respond to others, use language to communicate, grow cognitively, figure out why things work, embrace opportunities, and be motivated to learn more. It is through executive function that children manage thoughts, actions, and emotions to achieve goals (Miyake et al. 2000). Because of these important processes, the significance of executive function becomes a framework throughout this book, which, in turn, contributes to the important elements that foster and support resiliency.

Fostering Resilience

Kenneth Ginsburg and Martha Jablow's (2015) work speaks to the "7 Cs" of resiliency and their application to youth and teens.

In recent years, these experts have begun to tie their work back to the foundational years, which are fostered within early childhood program environments. In 2015 Gingsburg and Jablow identified these seven elements:

- Competence: learning how to do "what's right" but also learning how to recover when consequences from poor choices take place

- Confidence: feeling the thrill of "I can" but also the butterflies that come with feeling inadequate and the necessary thinking strategies to determine how to make confident choices

- Connection: experiencing opportunities to connect with not only peers but adults in healthy ways, as well as learning about supports that surround them in their community—good and bad

- Character: experiencing opportunities that provide a balance of "what's right" and "what's wrong" when interacting with people and the processes or materials that are involved in these experiences

- Contribution: experiencing opportunities to help and be helped with peers and adults in the environments that they are involved with each day

- Coping: navigating all the strong emotions that come with learning about feelings and what to do with each one in consistent and repetitive ways

- Control: experiencing opportunities to lead and follow while also practicing making choices—good and bad—with appropriate adult guidance

Each one of these elements is not an immediate know-how—meaning that we are not born with an innate ability to know what to do in each of these areas. They are developed and sculpted from *years* of experiences, both positive and negative, that mold who we are and that are hopefully supported in positive ways. What we know and will discover more within the book is that many of our most challenging children need extra energy and consideration to experience healthy positive and negative opportunities to cultivate these areas.

What We Can Do

To give children a fighting chance and to ultimately support necessary executive functions and resilience, we begin in chapter 2 with addressing the foundational pillars of environments that support children and families. This is followed by chapter 3's organizational systems overview with a focus on providing a balance of managing and overseeing, coaching and mentoring, and building and supporting community. The intent is to establish environments that are safe and consistent places that provide loving acceptance and kind intentions coupled with classroom activity that soothes and calms.

Chapters 4–7 present case scenarios of experiences we have had with children when working together and with others in the early childhood profession. In each chapter, we will see how the abstract idea of trauma directly and indirectly affects the individual child. Together we'll explore the consequences that events such as homelessness, incarceration, abandonment, medical emergencies, natural disasters, foster care, and atypical development have on children.

Last but by no means least, our final chapter will address the necessity of program staff to care for themselves before, during, and after the constant results of change in the lives of the children they care for. Through the delicate balance of continued focus on the theoretical framework presented in this chapter to the application of practical ideas and strategies all with the principles of executive function in mind, this book serves as a "must have" resource to use in individual as well as group environments serving young children who deserve a fighting chance.

CHAPTER 2

When Change Is Inevitable

The Pillars of a Supportive Classroom Environment

Early childhood programs that nurture relationships between caring adults and children have remarkable power to heal the lives of children experiencing significant change in their lives. Program environments are a key factor in the development of resiliency. This resiliency, or ability to recover from stress and trauma, involves creating and maintaining trust and comfort between children and adults. Galinsky's (2010) ideas of the seven life skills to promote executive functions of the brain assert that program environments assist children in learning ways to manage frustration, recognize and respond to others, use language to communicate, grow cognitively, figure out why things work, embrace opportunities, and be motivated to learn more. She notes that promoting these skills does not need to be done through expensive programs, materials, or equipment—it can be done through everyday interactions and activities. In this chapter, we'll address the foundational pillars necessary when supporting families and children to nurture resiliency in early childhood. A supportive early childhood program typically includes these important characteristics:

- leadership with appropriate vision and expectations suited to support developmentally appropriate, nurturing environments not only for children but for all individuals working within the environment

- classrooms that radiate a sense of security by using consistent daily routines to include designated adults working with children throughout the day in the program environment

- communication that is established and maintained among all significant adults in the child's life

- recognition of the impacts of touch and voice when used by adults and children throughout the day, emphasizing the connection to and trust of adults

- overall classroom arrangement with activity that uses visual schedules and appropriate transitions in between programs and/or classrooms

- classroom management that supports loving acceptance and kind intentions coupled with classroom activity that soothes and calms

Program environments are set up differently from state to state for a variety of reasons: government mandates, philosophies of child care, and physical space limitations, to name a few. Furthermore, program leaders surround themselves with daily caregivers who must embrace working with the families of today. To help explain the work that needs to be done with each child, Dr. Jane often uses the metaphor of an invisible bag. When children enter the program, they have an imaginary bag in each hand. Adults who have worked with children can determine what is inside those bags. Some children have bags filled with love and security. These children are engaged in the program; they talk about their home and classroom experiences, significant people in their lives, and daily activities of stable families and school environment. Their bags are weightless, and they can carry them easily.

Unfortunately, some children arrive with bags empty of love and security. These children are not engaged. Their invisible bags are instead a burden: they are filled with neglect, instability, or abuse. When these children reach into their invisible bags, they sometimes pull out aggressive words or actions. These children must lug and drag their heavy bags around with them. These bags clutter the floor and disrupt the room, taking up space while others trip over them.

It is up to the adults who work with children to determine how to manage the contents inside each child's bags. While you may not be able to completely relieve a child of his burdensome invisible bags, you can manage them. The first goal is to get them off the floor and out of the main areas of the classroom. In time, you may be able to help the child check those bags at the program door of the facility. This can help ensure the classroom is filled with warmth, acceptance, consistency, manageable stress, security, respect, and a commitment to one another.

Program Vision That Promotes Life Skills

We all know theoretically that program vision is important. But through years of leading a program and personal reflections, Dr. Jane has realized the importance of vision during her own journey. Hundreds of children have passed through her program, but it wasn't until recently that she began to have what she calls "full-circle moments." These moments arrive when you discover a child's entire life story and what has happened since the child has left your program. The making of these moments are at times costly: sleepless nights, frustration with parents, and endless dialogue with staff encouraging them to hang in there. But the payoff is grand—and shared vision is the essential element to the discovery of this important insight into the life of the child.

The need for support for early childhood has increased in the past few years. Staff members need connection to leadership, coworkers, and families. Parents seek more than a "how the day went" report. All parties are looking for more than what they are finding. Deb Curtis and Margie Carter discuss this search in the following excerpt:

> Within its control are buildings where people of different ages and, in many cases, different cultures come together each day with the potential of real interchanges of ideas, needs, skills, and resources. Everyone acknowledges that these children are our future. They represent our hopes, promises, and deepest longings. (2008, 16–17)

In chapter 1, we discussed how executive function evolves out of the seven essential life skills as determined by Galinsky's work. The challenge for early childhood professionals is to provide environments that allow children to learn ways to manage frustration, recognize and respond to others, use language to communicate, grow cognitively, figure out why things work, embrace opportunities, and be motivated to learn more. As the Center on the Developing Child (2011) notes, executive function skills are the crucial building blocks for the development of both cognitive and social capacities. Let's briefly look at each of these essential life skills and discover how day-to-day interactions can support their growth while also incorporating the tenets of vision:

- **Focus and self-control:** Let's face it, children and families are rushed, overscheduled, and stressed. This pressure taxes children's abilities to focus and concentrate. Infant teachers can foster focus by making eye contact and talking to a child while feeding her. Focus with older children might involve dress-up and role play with peers, promoting respect and acceptance.

- **Perspective taking:** A toddler is swinging around a baby doll that accidently hits a friend. A teacher can respond with "Ouch! The baby hit your friend, and it hurt her. Let's wash off the red place on Alyssa's arm together." A preschool teacher uses a weekly rotating helper chart to designate a morning and an afternoon line leader. This teacher might remind a preschooler who pushes others with "I know it is disappointing that you are not the leader this time, but your turn was yesterday, which was Wednesday afternoon. It will be your turn again on Friday."

- **Communicating:** While changing a baby's diaper, a teacher is warmly singing a song to the child. She is engaging the child with her eyes and facial features. In turn, the baby smiles and kicks in response to the teacher's labeling of the baby's excitement and movement to the song she is singing. In the preschool classroom, teachers encourage children to tell stories that the teacher writes down and gives to the children to illustrate. In either classroom environment, the teachers provide content-oriented activities each day that support learning letters, sounds, and the child's relation to the world.

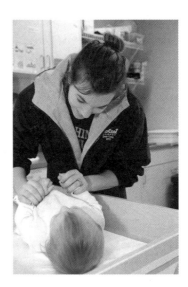

- **Making connections:** Teachers can read stories to babies and tod-dlers about four-legged animals. This leads to labeling those animals *dog*, *cat*, or *cow*, and then discovering that they make different sounds! The dog says "woof," the cat says "meow," and the cow says "moo." The preschoolers are learning that the number 1 means one object, the number 2 means two objects, and so forth. The activities cater to individual pace and comprehension level.

- **Critical thinking:** Classmates climb onto a slide and want to slide down but can't because the toddler at the bottom of the slide won't move. Everyone begins to fuss. The teacher intervenes before the fussing escalates and tells the toddler, "It looks like you need help being on the slide. Take my hand, and I'll help you to climb up for your turn to slide down." Everyone calms down and the process of play continues. Preschoolers learn to grow plants from seeds. The teacher allows the children to shovel the dirt, speculate about how much dirt it will take, the number of seeds, the depth in which to plant them, where to locate the potted plants in the classroom, when and how often to water, check on the plants, and chart the plant's growth. Whether growing a flower to give away, or growing a tomato to eat, the child must problem solve by sequencing, trying new processes, evaluating those processes, and seeing results and thinking about them because of the change they created.

- **Taking on challenges:** A two-year-old who is new to the classroom continues to cry when her mom leaves. By the third day, her crying is intense. One teacher in particular recognizes that the child responds to her more than the other teachers in the room. She approaches the child, calmly sits beside her, and labels with words how sad she is to see her mom leave. The teacher continues to talk calmly with her and engages others to bring her favorite book and stuffed animal from the book area. The teacher notices that the child seems to calm down when she rubs her back. After giving the child time to gather herself and readjust the high stress level she was experiencing, the teacher encourages her to engage with the classroom activity and transition into her day.

- **Self-directed, engaged learning:** When offered opportunities for give-and-take interactions, even infants begin to learn the foundation for engaged learning. This connection of being in sync with others creates interest and motivation to learn more—to be self-directed in figuring out how and why things work.

Each life skill discussed here depicts examples of opportunities to support the tenets of vision that a program director and staff believe and implement daily. The commitment by staff as well as their belief to use certain strategies and approaches are supported by leadership. These snapshots of interactions emphasize the importance of environments that provide trusting, caring adults who act as caregivers and role models. Even after controlling for socioeconomic status and IQ, research shows us that executive functions during early childhood are predictive of physical health, substance dependence, incarceration, and personal financial success at age thirty-two (Moffitt et al. 2011). The impact is lifelong and necessary to support the developing child who must also experience environments that have supportive rituals and routines that children can depend on, and lend support to their overall executive function.

The program should not be seen as just a safe place for children to stay while getting prepared to enter the school system one day. Children spend more of their waking hours in the program environment than with their families. The responsibility is immense and the partnership with parents paramount. Whether leading or teaching each day in the classroom, one must seize and align with others in the same space to create an environment that supports a vision of warmth, acceptance, consistency, manageable stress, security, respect, and commitment to one another. These tenets of vision then evolve into an environment and physical space that promote life skills.

Supportive Rituals and Routines

Family rituals and celebrations create memories that continue to build throughout a child's lifetime. A family child care provider shared how the children raced to the front window of her home each day to watch the workmen across the street build a home. At break time, the supervisor would honk his car horn and the men would stop and sit down and pull out their coffee cups and snacks. As the children watched this through the window of the provider's home for a few days, one of the older preschool children asked if they could have their morning snack at this time as well. When the horn sounded, the children would all sit together and

wait for their provider to bring their snack. Although the construction ended and the sound of the horn was replaced with a different cue, to the provider's delight, this ritual and daily routine was still taking place in her home *eight years later*, long after the children in her care at that time had grown and moved on. The powerful connections to such warm memories were passed down to each child who entered her home. An innocent opportunity created a lifetime of memories for the children in her care.

During these types of activities, children have a chance to bond, talk, problem solve, and share feelings with one another. As Howell and Reinhard (2015) so eloquently note, rituals add a meaningful dimension to routines, which gives children a sense of security when they need it most. These opportunities allow for them to see that adults can be trusted; adults will listen and support their ideas and wishes through healthy activities. Children create a sense of community when they see how people come together to enjoy one another's company.

Early childhood teachers can then extend this learning to a child's family and culture by creating opportunities within the curriculum and classroom planning. It is these types of activities that help children feel connected and part of a community family.

Communication between Adults

Children always need to experience communication between and by the significant adults in their lives. However, for children with disruptive change in their lives, communication by and between adults is imperative. It is important for early childhood professionals to have an awareness of cultural and socioeconomic backgrounds. They must also avoid using educational jargon and abbreviations, which can be confusing for children's parents. The last consideration is a commitment to using active listening. This strategy conveys to the child's parents that their insights are valued and their concerns and opinions matter. Active listening lays the foundation for mutual respect.

Impact of Touch and Voice

Children need adults who are mindful of the sensitivity of touch and voice. Touch encounters must include the following considerations: they are developmentally appropriate; the child's touch preference is respected, which includes recognizing that some children prefer touch on their backs and shoulders, while others can only tolerate touch minimally on their bodies. Adults should also provide overall assistance with helping children to understand bodies within a physical space.

Touch is supported by appropriate voice tone. Typically, harshly spoken words can have a negative effect on a child's overall behavior. A soothing voice provides opportunities to nurture and provide necessary security. Touch and voice are critical components for early childhood professionals to incorporate into the classroom environment.

Foundations of Classroom Arrangement and Management

Children find comfort in knowing what is going to take place on a consistent basis. So it's not surprising that an important aspect of promoting life skills is structuring the day to manage children's organization of time and space. Structure and organization should be layered within classrooms to provide opportunities for sensory play, explorations, discovery, and experiences with a range of materials and people. Environments that include the above-mentioned components set up the possibility of having clear, consistent expectations with the flexibility to respond to individual differences as well as allow and encourage multiage and peer relationships. These environments also allow the adults to be with the children fully by caring, teaching, and conversing rather than managing and instructing.

Time and space are organized by arranging the amount of space needed for children to complete an activity, the flow of traffic throughout the classroom, and the ability for the adults to supervise classroom activity. When determining space for activity centers, it is important to consider the number of children who will be able to participate at once. Fighting over turn taking and fussing about too little space can be controlled with visual cues children can easily identify.

For example, an adult can provide a certain number of smocks available in the art area or colorful Hawaiian leis purchased at the local dollar store for the book center. Children can see that the art area is full if all five smocks are in use or the book center is full when the leis are all being used. By wearing these items, children can clearly understand the limits of the space but know that they will have an opportunity to participate.

While security for children flows from being in a familiar space and predictable routines, this sense of safety also stems from a physical space that has these characteristics:

- provides opportunity for exploratory play

- addresses children's needs physically, cognitively, socially, and emotionally

- provides ample materials

- provides quiet spaces that have minimal stimulation

- provides pictures and labels at children's eye level that show children what to do in the activity area

- includes corresponding pictures and labels on shelves that remind children where each of the items in the center can be found and returned

- includes pictures that show positive behaviors that are supported in the classroom, such as children talking together to work things out or putting things where they belong in the classroom

- includes a visual daily schedule for all children that shows what to expect throughout the day

- provides personal spaces for each child, such as cubbies that are labeled with their names and belong just to them

Research shows that opportunities for sensory play, explorations, discovery, and experiences with a range of materials and people are important. The natural world is the first place to look for a rich environment (Greenman 2007). When outdoors, children experience the sun's rays, filtered light, blowing winds, drops of rain, and the smells of the earth. There are always ample materials and new places to explore.

By observing children as they move throughout the environment, teachers can gauge the positive or negative reactions children have to activities and environment elements. In addition, paying close attention to individual abilities allows teachers opportunities to adjust to match a child's needs and/or scaffold activities that support the child's learning at different levels.

Observing and noting individual differences can provide clear and consistent responses to children and encourage appropriate multiage and peer relationships. For children who struggle, a visual schedule to transition between programs and/or classrooms, and the daily routines of their classroom, is often helpful. Pairing with a peer and establishing communication between all significant adults in the child's life provides the necessary supports for struggling children. Here's how having a classroom management plan helps:

- It lets children know what they can do.

- It allows flexibility with rules and expectations.

- It acknowledges appropriate behaviors and interactions.

- It provides consistent limits.

- It provides opportunities to redirect.

- It delineates "safe" natural and logical consequences.

- It provides choices.

- It offers opportunities to reconnect when behaviors are inappropriate.

Recognizing the impacts of touch and voice when used by adults and children throughout the day emphasizes the importance of connecting with and trusting adults. Interestingly, planned interactions help to regulate distressing and out-of-control feelings in young children. Gentle rocking, a touch on the shoulder, a smile, eye contact throughout the day, simply standing still and holding a child are interactions that help to calm and get children back in control.

Opportunity for children to experience consistent, patient, tolerant, and caring interactions even when the child's actions are out of control can lead to calmer reactions. This speaks to the importance of the adults who must also manage their own feelings, impulses, and stressors.

Adults are the designers, planners, and constant evaluators of the environment that they are providing. Having access to beautiful buildings and the latest equipment doesn't create the best learning environment. The greatest lesson learned for many who lead programs is to recognize that it is the staff who provides the finest quality environments. Programs with committed staff members and quality teachers shine the brightest. Quality teachers set up environments that engage children by encouraging them to explore, play, discover, and think. Furthermore, children who have been traumatized thrive in environments where they experience calm and caring interactions with adults—those who nurture and connect to them.

Environment Pillars Can Determine a Life's Trajectory

We conclude this chapter with a full-circle moment that Dr. Jane experienced later on in her career. The experience centered on a child named "Megan." She was the baby who cried a lot, the child who refused to really connect with the teachers in the classroom, the daughter of a working, single mom who was riddled with guilt. Megan and her mom moved from place to place after enduring an ugly, angry divorce. Teachers recognized early that Megan was different. Feeding times were hard, diapering and toileting were challenging, and her ability to react and engage with others was limited.

Megan's mom would become angry and defensive when approached about teachers' concerns. She threatened several times to pull her child out of the program, while blaming teachers and other children in the classroom. Never, *ever*, was the issue centered on Megan and her developmental delays or family circumstances. Communication was frustrating and typically resulted in ongoing conflict. Finally, to everyone's relief, the day came for Megan and her mom to leave the program and enter into the local public school district never to be heard from again. But Megan resurfaced one day.

Dr. Jane began teaching an online class. When reviewing the class roster one fall semester, she spotted that familiar name from many years ago. Negative memories surfaced immediately. About three days into the class, Megan sent an e-mail: "Dr. H., are you really Ms. Jane?" It was 5:30 a.m., and as she sat in stunned silence, Dr. Jane thought, "Now her mom is going to track me down and tell me what a horrible college instructor I am!" Dr. Jane gathered herself and answered yes, she was Ms. Jane, and what a delight it was to see Megan grown and pursuing a college education.

To her surprise, Dr. Jane then received weekly e-mail messages from Megan. They included scanned pictures of Megan and her mom along with warmly written memories. Megan remembered the consistent care of the adults surrounding her and had fond memories of her interactions with them. To her, the classroom space "always felt like home," and she recalled the hugs and high fives and special traditions in the classrooms, as well as programming provided throughout the year. The same pictures that provided fond memories for Megan brought back difficult memories for Dr. Jane. At the end of the semester, Megan's mom asked Dr. Jane to call. The call turned out enlightening and rewarding. It started with "Remember all those years you all were trying to tell me that Megan had issues? You see, I didn't have what it took to listen at that point. However, in the first weeks of public school, I was jerked into reality, and services had to be developed for her along with a plan that has followed her to this day. I acted awful, and I am sorry, but know that because you and your staff hung in there for Megan and for me, she is the success that she is today."

We hope this full-circle moment inspires you to deliver *each day* to the children and families in your care. The lesson learned for Dr. Jane so many years ago was that she and the others at her program seized a collective vision of warmth, acceptance, consistency, manageable stress, security, respect, and commitment to one another and to the children and families they served. In addition, they provided opportunities for their children to experience life skills in the environments that included rituals and routines, appropriate classroom arrangement, and strong management classroom strategies. Megan was given a fighting chance and was set on a successful trajectory—one that was cultivated in her early childhood years. Megan, and the thousands of other children like her, *need* early childhood programs that embrace a collective vision to serve as their bedrock and that build the pillars of a supportive classroom environment. This strong foundation serves to nurture strong, happy children into eventually becoming strong, successful adults like Megan.

CHAPTER 3

The Program Perspective

A Team Committed to the Child and Family

So many early childhood programs are under considerable strain, having to withstand an incredible weight. This weight doesn't just include the immense responsibility of keeping children safe, secure, and loved in developmentally appropriate learning environments. No, programs must also meet the ever-increasing expectations of the significant adults in each child's life. In the past, teachers communicated with a small circle of adults for each child, perhaps the mom and dad and maybe a grandparent or two. In recent years, this circle has grown, in some cases, to several adults, including biological parents, stepparents, significant partners, and the resulting family that comes with a diversity of adult relationships. This circle can include grandparents, aunts, uncles, and others deemed important in the child's life. This diversity can create situations where adults perceive "ownership" of the child. Family dynamics can get complicated—fast! Whether predominantly positive or negative, it lands squarely on the shoulders of the early childhood teachers and program administrators to best navigate communication and ongoing relationships with the adults in each child's life.

For the early childhood professional, managing the many personalities that surround the child's home life becomes even more complicated when disruptive events take place. As we discussed in chapter 1, incarceration of a parent, substance abuse, living outside of nuclear family systems, varying mental health issues, and human-made or natural disasters are unfortunate trends that create complex issues in the lives of young children. It makes sense, then, for early childhood professionals to be informed about the home situations in order to develop strategies to best serve the children and adults in their families. This chapter's focus is to provide current, practical information and resources to ensure the early childhood professional team's success. A successful early childhood team recognizes disruptive change, works together as a team, seeks current research, and communicates with families regularly.

We would be remiss if we did not address the changing landscape of the early childhood education workforce. While we continue to work to change the nation's perception of child care, programs continue to be underfunded and underresourced. Lack of funding causes instability in program environments, teacher assignments, and program leadership. These changes hinder the continuity early childhood teams are capable of providing. While the funding problem cannot be solved in this book, it must be considered when planning a successful team approach to serving children with challenging disruptive life events. Positive role models in administration and in the classroom create the foundation to grow and sustain a quality early childhood program. In this chapter, you'll find ideas to provide a balance of managing and overseeing, coaching and mentoring, and building and supporting community. Margie Carter and Deb Curtis (2010) call this the triangle framework of counterbalances, and it clarifies a structure for supportive teamwork. As the team evolves, they find ways to navigate the many day-to-day challenges of children who are experiencing disruption in their lives. We begin by taking a closer look at the managing and overseeing side of the triangle.

PROGRAM VISION

Managing and Overseeing

Coaching and Mentoring

Building and Supporting Community

Managing and Overseeing

Leading or teaching each day in the early childhood program environment must be supported collectively by all individuals working within that space to support its structure. As discussed in chapter 2, a small program, such as a family child care home, or larger program environment first establishes and then revisits a collective vision. A vision, different from a mission statement, reflects the purpose of the program. A vision is the realization of how everyone interacts—not only within the program environment but beyond the classroom walls every day. Success in child care begins with a collective program vision that supports warmth, acceptance, consistency, manageable stress, security, respect, and commitment to one another. As Carter and Curtis (2010) stress, the program is driven by a group of people who collectively feel strongly about pedagogy and use the critical thinking skills necessary to constantly examine the assumptions they work within. These components support the larger organizational system that connects external environments, people, structure, processes, cultures, and outcomes.

Early childhood programs engage the greater world of activity in their communities. Each early childhood program can be divided into several components. In figure 1.1, we can see how Paula Bloom defines these components that make up a system as a whole:

Figure 1.1 Components of the System (Bloom, 2015)

Environment	People	Structure	Processes	Culture	Outcomes
The program receives funding, staff, and families from the outside, which, in turn, produce outcomes of program viability, satisfaction with work life, and parent satisfaction with their child's participation. The program is also viewed by the community as a viable business. The business must then navigate external environmental factors, such as child care licensing, food program compliance, work with competing programs in the area, and those interested in supporting children's advocacy efforts. External factors expect certain outcomes, which force the program to conform to standards that can be costly either monetarily or in regard to energy. This constant ebb and flow with outside factors creates a program that is an open system.	People bring their own values, attitudes, motivation, morale, and personal behavior to the program setting to work together. Each person has a role within the program environment, which shapes the culture of how people react and interact and grows to a collective personality.	The framework of the program must have several elements to work effectively. These include the legally required structure and program components; an organizational chart that distinguishes lines of authority; center policies, procedures, and parent handbooks; the overall vision and mission of the program, including the curriculum focus; and the physical building and setup.	This component consists of the actual day-to-day interactions between individuals working within the program's structure. It is the glue that allows for program activity to get completed every day.	What we mean by culture are the shared values, norms, history of the center, traditions, climate, and ethics that bring a group of people together to do the work that is necessary each day.	This component can be defined as the results of the people, structure, and processes that take place each day. It is the barometer of organizational effectiveness.

Notice that figure 1.2 outcomes vary and are measured in multiple ways. This data must be collected, monitored, and assessed on a regular basis so it can be used properly when making decisions concerning the organization's overall effectiveness. One of several resources mentioned within this book, Paula Bloom's *Blueprint for Action*, third edition, provides an online assessment tool called the *Early Childhood Work Environment Survey* (ECWES) that each staff member can complete. The ECWES provides insight into staff members' level of organizational commitment and their perception of the effort necessary to perform the work on behalf of the program, as well as their desire to work within the program. This tool assists by determining the collective commitment of the staff, and when completed periodically over time, it measures how commitment is fluctuating. Working to identify strengths and weaknesses of the program—especially

Figure 1.2 Early Childhood Centers as Organizations: A Social Systems Perspective (Bloom, 2015)

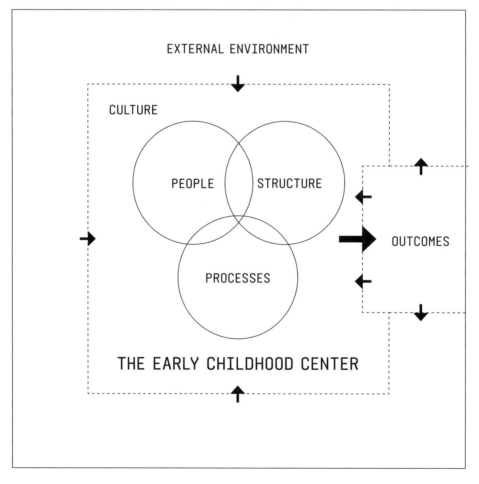

for those programs embracing work with challenging children—the process allows for individual staff members to obtain a better understanding of themselves as well as align themselves with others.

Many programs benefit when assessment tools are implemented. The assessment process allows everyone involved to better recognize the commitment necessary to do this work day in and day out, especially when serving children experiencing disruptive change. Being open to gathering information on a regular basis allows those within the program space to gain insight on all perspectives and obtain information to make decisions. The *Environment Rating Scales* by Harms, Cryer, and Clifford also provide excellent insight into supporting and providing quality environments for infants, toddlers, preschoolers, and school-age children. Each one of the designed scales assesses process quality that includes various interactions that take place in a classroom between staff and children, other staff, parents, and other adults. In addition, interactions among the children themselves are measured, which is indicative of the quality of materials, space, and schedule that support the children's activities. This can be tricky for the family child care home environment with limited opportunities to work with other adults within the setting to obtain another's perspective. Using the *Family Child Care Environment Rating Scale, Revised Edition* (FCCERS-R) also by Harms, Cryer, and Clifford, gives unique insight when providing an appropriate environment that serves multiple ages. Joining and participating in a local early childhood organization or online forum supports learning communities and provides professional development and networking with others.

Many states also provide child care resource and referral agencies and/or professional development initiatives to support family child care home providers as well as staff in larger programs.

Each of the suggested tools mentioned captures the global program environment, which includes looking individually at leadership abilities within the program as well as daily functioning in classroom environments. We can't emphasize enough that the practical ideas and strategies shared in later chapters will work more effectively if the program commits to seeking out, refining, and adhering to the quality of the organizational system to support developmentally appropriate practices and interactions between adults and children. Bloom (2015) emphasizes the importance for programs to do ongoing assessment, allowing for continued improvement efforts, conveying respect to staff, and encouraging a team approach to problem solving. Gathering and using this information to make adjustments among everyone encourages collaboration and fosters an environment that welcomes new ideas during times of change. Collaboration and flexibility are necessities when providing care to children and their

families experiencing disruptive change. Establishing and maintaining a style of communication that is effective and supports the processes within the overall organizational system is imperative for a successful program.

Communication Style and Positive Relationships

At the most basic level, even just implementing and maintaining daily contact between staff and parents, as well as upholding the many state and federal regulations and mandates, does not happen easily. The people in the program must function together with positive working relationships and communication styles. While the added element of working with children who are experiencing disruptive change in their lives presents its own level of complexities, the daily management and oversight of every program must address three distinct audiences who have different needs and perspectives: staff, parents, and administrators. When program staff have the following experiences, positive working relationships can be established and maintained:

- observing and experiencing a committed administration, especially when challenges arise

- feeling supported not only within the classroom but also when they are struggling—this includes being provided with helpful resources

- being informed about the day-to-day direction of the program, as well as knowing who to seek out should assistance be needed

- having ongoing opportunities to feel competent and trusted, which then builds confidence mastering the day-to-day reality of working in a classroom filled with busy children

For parents, the key aspects of positive communication take on a different perspective:

- being treated as equal partners when it comes to the care of their child

- being respected for their views on child-rearing practices

- being heard in regard to their need to learn and know more about their child's development and daily interactions

- being embraced, for better or worse, when difficult situations or misunderstandings take place

And finally, for those in administrative positions, your role in positive working relationships is much more active:

- Be aware and embrace that when challenges surface, a solution can be found—many times collectively.

- Understand that not one person is perfect, and until a staff member or parent proves differently, everyone should be trusted and treated equally.

- Listen actively and intently—model patience and understanding.

- Provide direction by using daily written and oral communication, and have a willingness to be that extra set of hands should issues arise in the classroom or with parents.

- Encourage others in leadership positions as they continue to learn how to lead and manage, while also supporting staff working in classrooms with busy children.

While these audiences have different roles, perspectives, and needs, relationships are based on effective communication strategies among the people working within the program. Another suggested tool by Bloom (2015) is *Communication Style*, which assists those working in small or large program environments to develop greater self-awareness and sensitivity to others. A deeper appreciation for how each person sends, receives, and interprets communication is a benefit of this assessment. Communication is critical to best serving children and their families, especially during challenging times, because interpersonal relationships and effective communication strategies are critical.

Communication opportunities have evolved over time. While still widely used, the note home is not the only go-to form of communication today. Many forms of communication are used in programs across the nation: in person, face-to-face discussions; phone conversations; FaceTime or Skype; e-mail messages; and text messages. The program staff should establish the most effective and confidential form for each family. Remember that nonverbal communication, such as facial expressions, eye contact, and body language, all convey intent and meaning. It is important to keep nonverbal communication as positive as possible. A two-way street of communication creates a sense of order, and people begin to feel competent as they build confidence when working and interacting with one another.

Managing Conflict

One of the first things to consider when dealing with conflict is to think about the atmosphere in which it is taking place. The atmosphere sets the tone for how everyone will agree, disagree, and build improved relationships. The goal is to promote positive interactions. To achieve that, consider the following elements:

- Believe conflict is not always negative.
- View resolution as a partnership.
- Maintain confidence.
- Have an open mind to solutions.
- Choose effective times to discuss and process.
- Avoid distractions.
- Provide locations that feel safe and comfortable.
- Nurture a spirit of cooperation.
- Concentrate on the issue at hand.
- Recognize that it is okay to agree to disagree.
- Maintain control of emotions.
- Use simple and respectful language.
- Be aware of perceptions.

As noted earlier in this chapter, when children are involved, it's easy for conflicts between the adults in children's lives to escalate. Generally speaking, if the adult relationships that surround the child are complex, there is a greater tendency for more emotionally charged conflicts, and many directors and teachers struggle with how best to approach tense situations. When effective communication strategies are implemented and maintained, many conflicts are resolved before they ever escalate.

Effective Communication

Remember the elements of dealing with conflict from the previous section? Working in the field of early childhood means constant human contact—and conflict is inevitable. Acknowledging conflict as a natural part of life and the program environment is often difficult for many people. Establishing expectations is key to success when facilitating effective communication.

Leadership must first establish that conflict is *not negative*. In fact, conflict can help to refine system processes and clarify understanding. A partnership approach by all of those involved can get to the root of an issue and create opportunity for problem solving and easing the situation at hand. Because issues that create conflict are complex, all the options to find a solution should be considered by everyone. Rarely is just one way of thinking or doing the answer to a problem. When everyone has an open mind to discussing potential solutions, we create opportunities to feel heard and be a part of a collective solution. As we will discuss in future chapters, rarely will the program staff, director, or parent have "the answer" to what is taking place with the child who is navigating disruptive change. A parent's recognition of what is taking place and its impact on his or her child can compound the issue. A parent may perceive the situation to be impacting only his or her circumstance. It is often helpful to gently acknowledge the impact on the entire family unit when everyone comes to the table to collectively determine solutions. Everyone needs to understand that solutions may need to change with the child's stage of development and the evolving disruptive life event. Providing "safe" spaces to discuss these ongoing circumstances will be an important consideration.

Meeting locations must have this in mind: comfort. Remember Dr. Jane's full-circle moment shared in chapter 2? Being contacted by a former student from years before brought immediate memories of unpleasantness when dealing with that child's parent. Those initial memories stirred up feelings of anxiety. Having to call together staff and parents to participate in a meeting about issues of concern can place everyone involved into anxiety overload. When we feel uncomfortable, the "fight or flight" response emerges. That's why engaging everyone to come to the table at times that are mutually agreed upon nurtures cooperation and sends messages that this is a collective effort to address what is taking place and that the focus of the meeting is to come up with solutions, with everyone's perspective considered.

When the group comes together, recognize that it will be okay to agree to disagree. Clarify expectations. This includes the director and teachers determining who will address certain issues. To that end, prepare an agenda with bulleted topics for the meeting as well as concrete examples to discuss. Being prepared helps people sort out what is feasible and really needs to be discussed. This agenda helps all participants to keep their emotions in check. Explicitly say up front, "Your child is important to all of us, or we wouldn't all be here today." When children are involved, many times the potential for issues to escalate happens quickly. A lesson learned so long ago by Dr. Jane in her full-circle moment was that she believed the ongoing perceived conflict with Megan's mom wasn't heading anywhere. But in reality, the conflict was planting seeds for the mom. After the explosive event took place with school personnel and after the family left her program, it finally "clicked" that something was indeed not quite right with Megan. Mom realized that seeking resources was imperative to assist Megan with her education. Essentially, Dr. Jane and her staff endured a five-year relationship because of their willingness to continue "hanging in there" with Megan and her mom. Trust and connection that withstood time was ultimately supported by the next side of the triangle, coaching, mentoring, and impactful adult learning opportunities.

Coaching and Mentoring

For teachers to learn more about children's social and emotional development and challenging behaviors, program leadership must support the people within the organizational system. In developing a plan for staff training, ongoing coaching and mentoring in the classroom should be part of the system.

How coaching and mentoring is done varies in many programs, with a variety of individuals providing this opportunity. Jablon, Dombro, and Johnsen (2014) note that coaching has been defined as helping individuals see themselves as effective while encouraging them to become motivated to use effective strategies in the classroom with intentionality to increase their competence. With so many quality rating systems in states across the nation, a significant focus has been placed on formal and informal educational experiences for adults working with young children. While many have embraced these learning opportunities, some in leadership positions have reported observing teachers waver when it comes time to implement what they have learned. Let's take a look at this scenario:

The director walks into the classroom to observe Ms. Patty and Ms. Lydia, who work together in the four-year-old classroom. Ms. Patty is the assistant teacher and has been working for the program for a little over a year. During that time, she and Ms. Lydia have been attending courses at the local community college. One of the most recent conversations in class was about the importance of allowing children to process a project with appropriate boundaries. Extended learning through allowing children to process creates and supports social-emotional development. Throughout the morning, Ms. Patty notices Rico and Oliver building "their town." They are excitedly building and working together to create a town of various places, including "their school." Almost every block and item in the block area becomes a part of Rico and Oliver's structure. Even more interesting, Oliver, who has been displaying several outbursts because of some changes within his family, is working cooperatively with Rico for the first time in a week. As Ms. Lydia gives the transitional signal for cleanup, both boys cry out, "We want to play with our town after nap. We don't want to tear it down." Ms. Patty instantly remembered conversations from class a few evenings before, and she tells the boys, "Let's rope off the area, and the two cots that are placed there can possibly be moved. We just need to talk with Juan and Corissa to make sure they are okay with their cots being in a different place for nap today." While nothing is said out loud, the director notices Ms. Lydia's glare at Ms. Patty. Lunchtime is not its usual chatter between children and teachers. As the children transition to nap, the director senses the stress and encourages a conversation between Ms.

Patty and Ms. Lydia. Ms. Patty begins the conversation with "I'm sorry if you felt that I overstepped my bounds. However, watching the two boys work together and seeing Oliver not have an outburst all morning long was such a relief. I just remembered from our class discussions the other night how important it is to respect children's work and extend the children's play, and I was delighted to see Oliver have a morning where he was focused and engaged." "Really," snaps Ms. Lydia, "now all the children will want to leave their work lying around, and we will never have a sense of order in our classroom!" She goes on to say, "I wish that our college professor spent just one day working with these children—she would see just how hard it really is!" Both teachers turn and look to the director for input and support.

Stepping outside of the day-to-day administrative processes that must be completed in order to coach and mentor is a delicate dance that, frankly, sometimes feels impossible. Becoming a coach and mentor is a role for those in administrative positions as well as for seasoned teaching staff perceived by others as mentors. Having the ability to nurture others' talents and abilities strengthens the organization overall. And it all begins with recognizing the different types of learning styles:

- **Visual learners** have a tendency to take things in through watching and reading first and then choosing to participate.

- **Auditory learners** need to hear about issues and talk about them first before choosing to participate.

- **Kinesthetic learners** must move around, touch, and feel; they will participate as long as they can keep moving.

A final resource that this director could seek out from Bloom's (2015) collection is *Learning Style*. Having an awareness of each teacher's learning style can not only recognize but help identify possible clash points. For example, if Ms. Lydia was a visual person, accepting that a space within the classroom will not have the "normal look," based on the classroom schedule, is upsetting. Hearing why it was important to support the boys from the auditory-dominate person, Ms. Patty, was frustrating for her. While Ms. Lydia heard in class why it was important, she had difficulty "seeing" why this was important. From the director's standpoint, recognizing and respecting the style of learning gives subtle hints to consider. Offering to be available after nap to observe together how the boys respond to the opportunity allows Ms. Lydia to see if the opportunity extends the children's learning as well as supports Oliver's recent challenging behaviors. The director also discussed with Ms. Patty about setting appropriate boundaries with Rico and Oliver once they awoke from nap. One boundary included taking a picture of "their town" to be displayed in the classroom, but they would need to put everything away by the end of the day. As the afternoon wore on, Ms. Lydia was able to observe an engaged Oliver including additional children in on the fun. The digital picture to add to the collection of class work was also a nice added touch and a visual reminder for Ms. Lydia of the successful event. Unless teachers have an awareness of learning styles, most well-intentioned opportunities for children in the classroom and the director's ability to create and sustain relationships between coach and mentor can easily spin out of control. While recognizing individual learning styles is important, we must also understand how we learn as adults.

Adult Learning

In any mentoring-coaching relationship, both persons must understand the basic tenets of adult learning. These principles, as shared by Merriam, Caffarella, and Baumgartner (1999), add meaning and insight to the learning processes necessary to the professional growth of adults working in the early childhood field:

- **Self-directed learning:** Adults want to learn about concepts that are relevant to their lives and current situations.

- **Motivational theory:** This theory notes a strong link between the willingness to participate in a learning activity and achieving a goal.

- **Critical reflection:** Individuals reflect on new knowledge and its relevance and application to their everyday use and interactions.

- **Transformative learning:** Working in tandem with reflection, the learner not only tests out the new concept but adapts it for use in his practice.

Fortunately for this director, both Ms. Patty and Ms. Lydia are motivated to attend classes at the community college. Because of this commitment to be lifelong learners, the director can serve as a sounding board for new learning by connecting course content to everyday experiences. The teachers' motivation to take advantage of role modeling and mentorship opportunities increases with support of their director. Energy that can then be connected to the third and final side of the triangle supports both the environment and cultural aspect of the overall organizational system.

Building and Supporting Community

When the director and staff commit to working with children on behalf of the community, staff members are charged with engaging families and outside entities, such as neighboring schools, businesses, and other professionals. Here's how to create that relationship (Carter and Curtis 2010):

- Facilitate an environment that creates a sense of belonging.

- Recognize and respect individual contributions.

- Create a shared vision between staff and families.

- Nurture a bond between all individuals working within the program environment.

- Understand the cultural contexts of staff and families.

- Encourage shared experiences that continue to enhance the ongoing history taking place at the program each day.

- Connect those who work within or attend the program to outside resources as they are needed.

We are living in a time when adults, including teachers and parents, are rushed and stressed—and often we are quick to create a cycle of doing things for children rather than stopping to teach and role model independent behavior. Repeating the cycle only encourages children to move away from wanting to contribute to "the greater good" and often results in children losing a sense of belonging to a community. This cycle, compounded with a significant disruptive event, leads to early childhood programs dealing with frustrated and angry children. A feeling of not being worthy is a common theme among children stuck in this cycle. An environment that creates a sense of belonging with intentional teaching practices becomes important.

Those working with high-risk children and families often report that one of the most glowing attributes early childhood professionals possess is to teach children with intentionality and to ensure that children feel safe. This act of intentional teaching means to act purposefully with a goal in mind. As Epstein (2007) has found, intentional teachers create clearly defined learning objectives while also assessing a child's progress by modifying activities as needed. This includes a balancing act of child-guided and teacher-guided activities that partners with an environment that provides safety.

Intentional teaching allows children to pay attention and focus. For example, children who are homeless may not know how to properly sit at a table, eat with utensils, and consume the food offered in a relaxed manner. It is the intentional teacher who may initially need to model and direct while also carefully watching and observing the child's abilities to acquire the skills. What may start out as a hand-over-hand process may then result in a simple classroom transition time to sit and eat with peers while engaging in purposeful conversations with teacher and peers. While we often assume that everyone knows how to come and eat at the table, children experiencing homelessness may have rarely had opportunities to create an eating norm. Intentional teachers make thoughtful choices about the classroom environment, curriculum activities, and student interaction.

Two ingredients are necessary when recognizing and respecting individual contributions to include: (1) program environments that are supported by consistent routines and (2) teachers who are supported to be "fully present" when working with the children in their care. As Schiller (2009) encourages, routines help staff, children, and families feel safe, and being "fully present" means that teachers take the time to listen to each child's comments and statements. Everyone within the program space learns they can depend on the environment; this lends to feelings of being in control and an awareness of what is coming next. Continuity within a program builds trust, which is the ultimate foundation of social and emotional intelligence and supports cognitive growth and development. With time and consistency, these ingredients encourage children to participate in cooperative play by using materials, interacting with others, and contributing with intentionality to support the greater community that is cultivated.

Capturing the organizational system structure and cultural context includes the process of writing policies and guidelines that set forth the expectations of the program. Parent handbooks and center policy handbooks must reflect fair, equitable, and antibias policies being practiced on a daily basis. A foundation to consider when designing principles to support an understanding of how the program will approach developmentally appropriate practices when providing guidance to young children within the program model includes these suggestions (Hemmeter 2007):

- Recognize that children are in the process of learning acceptable behavior.

- Effective guidance approaches are preventative because they respect feelings while addressing behavior.

- Adults must seek to understand reasons for a child's behavior.

- Supportive relationships between children and adults are the most critical component of effective guidance.

- Adults must use guidance methods that help children learn self-control and responsiveness to the needs of others.

- Modeling appropriate expressions of feelings by adults is important.

- Adjustments to a child's environment or schedule are necessary to meet his or her needs.

Coupling these principles with equipment and material choices should also reflect an appropriate flavor of culture and diversity. Encourage ongoing conversations among staff and parents, and stay in tune with the ever-evolving diversity and flavor of culture to strengthen relationships within the program. The final area of consideration is connecting to the greater community of professionals.

Every community has a wealth of resources available to assist families and early childhood professionals. As stated earlier, work with children who are experiencing disruptive change in their lives has become a norm. Directors and teachers are reporting the need to access specialists for families, including professionals with expertise in social work, mental health, and the medical community. Some of these medical professionals include the following:

- early childhood/child development specialists

- behavioral health therapists/counselors

- pediatricians

- speech-language pathologists

- audiologists

- occupational therapists

- physical therapists

Early childhood mental health consultants have also become another effective resource. Research shows access to early childhood mental health professionals reduces expulsions and documents improvements in children's behaviors and teacher attitudes and overall classroom behaviors (Perry, Allen, Brennan, and Bradley 2010). Early access to consultation services and the establishing of a collaborative relationship between consultant, program, and family focuses much needed energy on making choices that support the child through the disruptive event taking place in his life.

While this chapter has shared many practical resources to help program leaders refine their organizational systems, it is important to discern that a shared visioning process goes beyond the use of checklists and tools. A vision allows for everyone within the program, including parents and children, to deepen personal connections that radiates into the greater community. Dr. Jane was able to observe the remarkable connection the families in her program had not only with the staff but with each other over time. Recent years have found her families contacting her and other staff members via online social networks to share how they are doing and to share connections they still had with friends from their preschool days together. Balancing the overall organizational system included numerous parent meetings, coffees, and other social events that created and sustained support networks, acknowledged family expertise, shared power and decision making, strengthened the appreciation of diversity, and provided communication opportunities for information sharing between families and the program. Additionally, staff members have shared fond memories of cultivated friendships that, outside of the workplace, have provided support through good and bad times over the years.

We hope the first three chapters provided a wealth of information and insight for creating successful child care environments. Key elements for a successful program include a context of theoretical foundations; program environment fundamentals for small and large programs; and organizational system elements that provide support in the areas of managing and overseeing, coaching and mentoring, and building and supporting community. The next several chapters allow the reader to apply the provided foundation of information while exploring practical strategies used to assist children who have experienced disruptive change in their lives. This includes children experiencing homelessness, parent incarceration, multiple parent relationships, loss of a parent, a natural disaster, foster care, and the medical diagnosis of a sibling.

CHAPTER 4

Homelessness and Parental Incarceration

A Fighting Chance for Gracie and Quinton

A s chapter 1 established, early childhood professionals serve children who have experienced disruptive events in their lives best when they implement the following practical ideas and strategies:

- Establish consistent communication between the significant adults in a child's life.

- Provide consistent warm responses to behaviors within the classroom with carefully planned activities.

- Commit to provide each child who is struggling an informed, coordinated, calm, and nurturing environment.

- Access information and resources to increase personal knowledge and understanding.

In this chapter, you will see the real-life stories of children and families going through two scenarios of major disruptive change. Along with these stories, we will share practical strategies and ideas for managing disruptive change in these children's lives, including an overview based on the many tenets discussed in the first three chapters. Be sure to reference the appendix for the lists of resources to use when issues arise. As we talk about each of these children and what disruptive changes he or she is going through, we address getting outside consultations, interventions, and specialized service providers. We encourage you to explore resources in your community and surrounding areas. And most importantly, all who are involved must be *willing to embrace* disruptive change in the lives of children, address it with professionalism, and consistently use a complement of suggested activities and ideas, recognizing that what may work one day may not work the next. Flexibility becomes a necessary ingredient for success. All strategies should be couched within developmentally appropriate environments to provide the necessary stability in the lives of these children.

The first case focuses on Gracie. Gracie is reeling from the effects of homelessness that have had an impact on her life and the lives of her family members. In the second case, we will discuss Quinton, the child of an incarcerated parent. As with these children and the others described in the following chapters, we will examine how a child's executive function—which brings together feelings and thinking, and supports our ability to reflect, analyze, plan, and evaluate—is affected in each situation. Children in situations similar to the first two particular cases, as with most children experiencing disruptive change, can exhibit behaviors that could be developmentally appropriate for their age. Please note that while these behaviors may be considered appropriate, it is the intensity and duration of the behaviors of the children discussed that sets these children apart from their peers. Furthermore, acute changes in destructive behavior is a red flag, signaling the need for exploration and observation, as well as a referral and work with other community professionals.

Gracie's Disruptive Change: Homelessness

One of the child care centers that Kari worked with was located in a low-income area known for homelessness and crime. The director had been the administrator for a little over eight months, and the teachers had been working together in the same classroom for about four months. One teacher had completed the requirements for a Child Development Associate (CDA) credential, and another was in the process of obtaining an associate's degree in child development at the local community college. When asked about ongoing professional development opportunities for both her and the staff, the director acknowledged that she was still trying to determine the strengths and weaknesses of her staff to establish a balance between teaching teams. Both the director and teachers reported working well together, and Kari's early observations supported this. As conversations evolved, it was evident that the team appeared open to suggestions. Though the center was a smaller facility, its director and teachers were committed to continuity of care and were invested in the lives of the children and families served.

As Kari began her consultation, the director and teachers met with her and discussed problems that had arisen and continued over a three-week period. The lead teacher in the two-year-olds classroom, Susan, reported that one child was living at the shelter a few blocks from the child care center. Gracie's family had been evicted from their home and were living with a number of family members until they moved to the shelter. Susan reported that the mom and dad were still bringing Gracie and her siblings regularly to child care while they continued to seek out other living arrangements. Gracie had been attending this child care center daily since she was six weeks old. The teachers reported that Gracie was typically a good child. She followed directions well, played with many of her friends in class, and was always the first to sleep at naptime. Everyone agreed that this felt like a one-time, or acute, trauma event for Gracie.

Over the three-week period since moving to the shelter, Gracie's behavior had changed. She refused to join in group activities, hit and bit other children, did not sleep at naptime, and disrupted other children trying to sleep. Teachers also noted that Gracie had been having a hard time transitioning into the classroom at drop-off and would cry for her mom and dad for an hour after they left. Through conversations with Kari, the teachers saw that, while they were unable to provide stability in Gracie's living situation, they could—and did—commit to providing stability while she was in their care. It was important to the teachers that the activities and intervention strategies they implemented revolved around providing stability and consistency and giving some sense of control to Gracie. Most importantly, the teachers and director made a commitment to Gracie and her family to provide a safe space physically as well as emotionally—a place where Gracie could feel safe expressing her emotions, where teachers labeled emotions and realized they could not fix Gracie's problems.

Before any classroom activities were changed, the director arranged to have a meeting with Gracie's parents. She began by acknowledging what major change had happened within their living conditions and gave some concrete examples of how Gracie's behaviors had changed in the classroom. Because the director emphasized how she and the teaching staff viewed them as equal partners, Gracie's parents were willing to support the classroom recommendations, as well as incorporate some of the suggestions into their current living conditions. Ultimately, sharing communication about the family's next steps was seen as essential, and doing so created an opportunity for the director and staff to make additional referrals to community resources to help the family reestablish continuity in their lives.

Improving Executive Function

As the team met with Kari, they shared their observations and determined they could help Gracie by amping up the predictability and consistency in her day. According to Zysk and Notbohm (2010), children who know what to expect and how teachers and peers are going to react can predict most of their day and become more successful in the classroom. Because of Gracie's age, it was apparent that the strategies needed to be developmentally appropriate and benefit not only her but the other two-year-olds in the classroom as well. Through the following strategies and activities, Gracie's behaviors began to slowly change and her executive function was enhanced:

- Predictability: The initial step was to create a strong sense of predictability within the classroom that provided a safe place for the children overall. Once a daily routine was established in the earlier team meetings with the director, the teachers adhered to it as closely as they could, warned Gracie of changes, and talked through that change and how they were going to get back on schedule. This allowed Gracie to work on her ability to **focus** and learn, while also supporting her ability to learn **self-control**.

- Teacher picture board: Knowing who was in the classroom at arrival and throughout the day became very important to Gracie. The transitions between opening teachers, floating teachers, and closing teachers became difficult for Gracie. She would throw tantrums, become more physically aggressive, and cry during these times. The staff decided to use picture boards outside all the classrooms. Each board had a picture of who was in the classroom during the morning routine, the lunch routine, and the closing routine. The director decided to hire two full-time substitute teachers who would give teachers breaks and cover lunchtimes. The substitute teachers would also be able to develop relationships with all the children and help with stability and predictability in the classroom. Gracie learned how to **take on a challenge** by using the picture board to manage the change of teachers throughout the day.

- Visual schedules: The teachers collected resources to help design and implement visual schedules for the classroom. The teachers started with a simple visual schedule to use during drop-off. They used a First/Then schedule and took pictures of Gracie doing routine activities around the classroom and facility. Gracie would hold her visual schedule that had a picture of her waving to her parents, and then she would choose from two picture cards to determine what she was going to do next. This allowed her to have control over what she was going to do next, nurturing a sense of security. Her **critical-thinking** skills were enhanced as well since she had to study and apply the steps provided in the visual schedule.

- Supported peer interaction: Since Gracie had been a very social toddler and had only recently begun to exhibit aggressive behaviors, providing supported interaction was helpful. The teacher had Gracie do a structured play activity with one peer at a time. Gracie loved puzzles, so she, a friend, and the teacher sat at the table and put together a puzzle and then traded  puzzles with other children. Gracie resisted trading at first but did so after she got used to the idea. This strategy was extended to other play opportunities, such as climbing on the play structure outdoors, caring for a hurt friend who was crying, and sharing toys at the sensory table, which was another favorite play area for Gracie. The way the teacher supported play between friends in the classroom environment enhanced Gracie's **perspective-taking** abilities.

- Biting diary: The classroom teachers kept a biting diary to observe and record what happened when a bite took place and what was happening in the environment when the incident took place. To determine Gracie's habits, Kari also observed during the times of day when Gracie's biting seemed to increase. Gracie's biting and aggressive behaviors had a distinct pattern. She would bite during center time when three or more children were with her at a particular center. She would bite during outside play when three or more children were on the slide with her, in the sandbox with her, or playing with large-motor toys. Mealtime was also a biting time, as Gracie was seated at the table with her peers.

  ‣ Whenever too many children got near Gracie, she would bite and hit others to get them to go away. Teachers planned center time and used the visual schedule with the class to manage the number of children in each center. Outside play was also more structured, and children were encouraged to do other activities when it got too crowded. Mealtime was an easy fix. Gracie was moved to a smaller table with one or two friends. She sat at the end of the table and not in the middle, and she also sat with her back to the children at the large table. By using the biting diary, the teachers were able to pinpoint times when Gracie's **focus and self-control** needed assistance and support.

- Expressing anger: Throughout the day, Gracie exhibited a wide range of emotions. The staff made one corner of the classroom into a cool-off spot for all the children. The cool-off spot was visible to the teachers. A rocking chair, books, a Get It Back Together Bag (see "Classroom Resources" in appendix), and other activities were available for children to experience and to use to "get the mad out." When the teachers saw Gracie or another child getting angry, they took the child to the cool-off spot and remained with her or him if the child wanted them, or encouraged use of the activities designed to help. Many children were able to use the cool-off spot, and biting and hitting decreased over time. This assisted not only Gracie but her classmates when practicing the skills necessary to support **perspective taking**.

Holistic Program Support

Notice that each of the previously mentioned strategies were implemented over time in the classroom. In addition, as Kari listened to the director, she suggested that the director and the staff consider completing Bloom's *Early Childhood Work Environment Survey* (ECWES), as discussed in chapter 3. This would provide insight into each person's level of organizational commitment and her perception of the effort necessary to perform the work on behalf of the program. Having a better gauge of her program would allow the director to see the collective commitment of the staff and provide a baseline from which to build the entire program's organizational system. The classroom teachers needed just a bit more help in strengthening the overall organization and management of their rooms. Accessing Bloom's "Infant-Toddler Teaching Practices" in *Blueprint for Action*, third edition, helped the teachers focus on assessing their teaching practices, while also taking a closer look at the classroom environment with help from the director. Additional resources and materials were purchased, and children's books on the subject of homelessness (see p. 129) were incorporated into the library area and circle times. These new items and the small changes benefited all of the children.

In regard to overall communication, the director and teaching staff reported feeling better about Gracie's progress, as well as the atmosphere of the entire classroom. While some days were better than others, everyone continued to be committed to assisting Gracie through this disruptive change. In addition, they talked regularly to process their concerns for her family, and ongoing communication

with her parents eventually resulted in them finding housing. This acute trauma event for Gracie was acknowledged and managed by the many adults invested in her life, but the next story proves to be a bit more complicated.

Quinton's Disruptive Change: Parent Incarceration

The next program to experience a major complex trauma event centered on a child named Quinton and his family. A four-year-old, he attended a large child care facility and was in the preschool class with Ms. Barbara and her teaching partner, Mr. Charles. The program's director had been at the location for several years, while both teachers had been on the team for the past couple of years. Early observations showed several changes in the adults who were bringing Quinton to school, along with odd phone calls during the day from Quinton's grandmother, Marcy, inquiring about how he was doing. The phone calls were quick, with little information being shared by the grandmother.

The teaching team requested a meeting with the director. Ms. Barbara reported that Quinton had been acting out more and disrupting her typically calm classroom. He had become increasingly aggressive, hitting and biting his peers. He was also more impulsive and had been having tantrums during each transition, especially at drop-off and pickup at the end of the day. In addition, he was very clingy to Mr. Charles, much more than usual, and was panicky if he looked around the room and could not see him. The teachers and director thought it necessary not only to talk with his parents but also to consider referring Quinton to a local counselor who specialized in early childhood for a screening. Ms.

Barbara offered to take the lead since she felt she had established a relationship with Quinton's grandmother.

After talking with his grandmother, Marcy, Ms. Barbara discovered that Quinton had moved in with his maternal grandparents very recently, during a weekend. Marcy shared that Quinton's parents were involved in a domestic violence situation, and his mother had to stay in the hospital while Quinton's father went to jail. Both of his maternal grandparents expressed concern about Quinton and his change in behavior. A once gentle, compliant child had turned into an aggressive, angry child. Marcy also expressed her anxiety, fear, and anger toward Quinton's father and his mother. His mother was making choices that Marcy thought weren't healthy or appropriate. Upon Ms. Barbara's request, Marcy agreed to come in and meet with both the director and teachers. Concern about his initial reactions and risky behavior and its consequences later in childhood were certainly at the forefront of his teacher's and family's minds—no one truly knew what Quinton had witnessed or experienced during his parents' domestic dispute.

As the director and teachers met to discuss the information that Ms. Barbara had discovered and plan for the meeting with Marcy, they agreed that it would be critical to first identify the emotions both Marcy and the teachers were dealing with. Maintaining professional boundaries by listening but not overreacting to the situation was key. What the director and teachers could control was what happened during the hours that Quinton was spending with them. What took place outside of those hours was important but dependent on the support his grandparents gave him. The staff wanted to emphasize the importance of maintaining continuity at the program by Quinton coming and leaving at the same time each day. They also wanted to express the importance of daily communication about how he was doing both in the home and early childhood program environment.

At the meeting, the director led with their predetermined talking points. The meeting was held in the classroom at the end of the day. The teachers wanted Quinton's grandparents to feel comfortable and to better understand the setup of their classroom, as well as where his things were located, where he slept during naptime, and the overall classroom activity throughout the week. During the meeting, the topic of Quinton's mother was brought up. While the consequences of what had taken place between Quinton's parents were still playing out, the teachers and his grandparents felt that Quinton's mother should press charges and choose to live with her son instead of with his father. Knowing and dealing with those feelings by talking openly about it allowed everyone to be on the same page when coming up with strategies to assist Quinton, both in the short term as well as long term. Because of the sensitivity of the issue and the knowledge that several variables were out of the control of everyone present, the meeting's focus was to ultimately try to help Quinton achieve a behavioral equilibrium while he was at the program. The staff also wanted to lend support and ideas to the grandparents who were now in the parental role. The grandparents were also open to seeking assistance from the local counselor who was recommended and had pursued an appointment with her.

Improving Executive Function

Throughout the meeting, the group discussed that Quinton's behavior was problematic at home as well as in child care. He was impulsive—grabbing toys and other children—and aggressive—hitting and biting other children and staff. He had numerous temper tantrums throughout his day. He also began to reenact the violence that he witnessed by hitting toys and saying adult phrases. He also expressed that he missed his mom and dad and would cry frequently throughout his day in child care and at his grandparents' house. Through the meeting, the staff and grandparents developed a plan to help Quinton during the time he spent in child care and the time he spent at home with his grandparents. To do this, the adults needed to focus on building and teaching coping skills to Quinton. Reassurance, consistency, and routines were also added into the plan. The results of the meeting included specific ways the family and child care teachers were able to help Quinton and support his executive functioning:

- Postcards: Quinton expressed many emotions about his mother and father. Mostly, he missed them. His grandparents made pre-addressed postcards and crayons available to him as soon as he got home from child care. This activity was added into his routine, and he was able to write and color as much or as little as he wanted. Ms. Barbara also provided Quinton the opportunity to send his parents pictures he completed in the art center, or Ms. Barbara wrote letters for him. Marcy added a trip to the post office on Saturdays to mail his work to his parents. This activity provided Quinton with a safe way to communicate with his parents while giving him some control over his life. He wrote or colored, stamped, and put the letters or postcards into the mailbox at the post office. Quinton was learning how to **make connections** by having support to express himself with letters and words.

- Picture play: Quinton seemed to gravitate to the art center every day. He would write to his parents, but he also would draw and color

pictures. Quinton drew pictures, and Mr. Charles talked to him about what he drew. He labeled pictures for him. The pictures he drew were often of the violence he witnessed in his home. He was allowed to draw these; Mr. Charles responded calmly and did not ask questions about specific events but rather commented on the colors or shapes. Mr. Charles was supporting Quinton's **focus and self-control** by providing an outlet for his feelings while also being present as Quinton processed the life events that were having an impact on him.

- Phone contact: Marcy kept in contact with her daughter, Quinton's mother. Legal requirements meant Quinton was able to talk to his mother on the same day at the same time each week. He was able to tell his mother about his week and activities at school. She was able to comment on the artwork he sent to her. Marcy was very clear about boundaries, and his mother was aware that talk of visits and overnight stays were not something to be discussed. If Quinton asked when he would get to see his mom, the adults would tell him the next date for supervised visitation. Consistency in contact was important to developing coping skills for Quinton as well as supporting appropriate outlets for **communicating**.

- Reassurance: Worry and anxiety about his father and his care was something Quinton talked about frequently at child care and at his grandparents' home. He worried that his dad was not being taken care of and given food. He worried about his dad not having a blanket or somewhere to sleep at night. His teachers and grandparents reassured him that his father was being taken care of and provided for. The local newspaper provided statistics for the detention center and even provided a menu of what was served at each meal. His grandparents read the menu to Quinton whenever he asked about his dad being hungry. They also checked out books from the local library that specialized on the topic of parent incarceration (see pp. 129–130) and read to him while also offering items within a sensory basket to help soothe him while he enjoyed books. This allowed Quinton the opportunity to **make connections** with the support of the adults who were explaining about his dad's care at the prison.

Holistic Program Support

Luckily for Quinton, he attended a program where the director and teachers collectively worked together with a vision and expectations suited to support developmentally appropriate, nurturing environments for the children and families. They focused on providing a classroom that radiated a sense of security by using consistent daily routines that Ms. Barbara and Mr. Charles supported. Because the teachers and director were prepared and acknowledged the sensitivity of the issue, the meeting with the grandparents established and maintained communication between all significant adults in Quinton's life. By being available to him, all the adults were able to appropriately support Quinton by listening and labeling his feelings. Quinton, in turn, had the opportunity to connect with and trust adults. Through the teachers' use of appropriate classroom arrangement and management, Quinton was able to be in a space that provided activity that was able to soothe and calm. Helping Quinton learn coping skills and learn how to express his emotions, no matter how scary, went a long way in building successful life skills for this child.

More Considerations

For Gracie and Quinton, recognition of what was developmentally appropriate for their ages was considered. When looking back at the information shared in chapter 1 concerning child trauma and toxic stress, we see that Quinton was certainly at higher risk because of his circumstances and the complex trauma he was experiencing. However, that does not discount Gracie's acute event, as both children needed support from the adults in their lives. It is also important to consider the impact the events had in relation to the ACEs study, specifically for Quinton. The subject of domestic violence and abuse has been studied immensely. Based on information gleaned from the ACEs study, male children witnessing domestic violence against their mothers are at 70 percent greater risk than their peers for fathering children during their teen years (Moore and Ramirez 2015).

The research behind Strengthening Families allowed both families to benefit from the efforts displayed by the staff (Harper Browne 2014). Gracie and her family were supported by resources to help locate a place to live, while Quinton's grandparents were supported by the referral to a local counselor who specialized in early childhood issues. Each was nurtured to bounce forward rather than backward when faced with their disruptive change events. Both families were referred to community resources, and information was shared to increase parenting and child development. Most importantly, the programs were working to provide classrooms and organizational systems that supported positive social and emotional competence for all of the children to include their executive function and resiliency.

CHAPTER 5

Multiple Parent Relationships and Death of a Parent

A Fighting Chance for Taylor and Tate, and Jasmine and Noah

P art of this chapter's focus on twins Taylor and Tate was first published in an article written for *Child Care Exchange* (Humphries and Rains 2015). Dr. Jane and Kari provided insights into the twins' lives as they faced disruptions in their care by primary adults outside of the early childhood program, including the chaos of changing living situations, caregiver entry into or exit from their lives, and financial strain. This chapter will go on to explore two other circumstances for children who are experiencing the death of a parent—Jasmine's by community violence, Noah's by a sudden, unexpected death. These real-life stories capture how the directors and teachers within these programs realized that the consistent and caring early childhood program offered the most stable environment in these children's lives. The flood of emotions displayed by the children in this chapter required a sensitive and knowledgeable adult within the classroom. Because of the importance of this support for healthy social emotional expression, the discussion emphasizes activities to use with a balance of practical strategies that continue to support executive functioning. Children are capable, and building on their capacities is necessary (Galinsky 2010). With a focus on death of a parent, this chapter will also apply several of the 7 Cs of resiliency as discussed in chapter 1. Be sure to reference the appendix for the lists of resources to use when issues arise.

Taylor And Tate's Disruptive Change: Multiple Parent Relationships

Taylor and Tate began acting out during routine activities in the classroom. Drop-off, pickup, and circle times were occasions for extreme negative behavior: biting and difficulty participating in activities. At mealtimes, they grabbed other children's food, pushed chairs over, and yelled. To complicate matters, the teachers in the classroom felt caught in the middle of the twins' parents. Their divorce, which was quite ugly, resulted in very tense relations. The twins' mom had been having an outside relationship, which was the catalyst for the divorce. It also meant the twins' father wasn't willing to cooperate with anything that had to do with the mom and her new boyfriend. The teachers and director, who had a longtime relationship with the family and had cared for the twins since they were infants, were also quite disappointed in mom's choice to seek the outside relationship, since they adored the twins' father. The twins' mom felt the disappointment and became defensive on anything related to the twins' care. When the director approached her about the mounting tuition bill, she snapped back with "That's their dad's problem—tell him to read the divorce decree" and stormed out. On the days that the dad picked up the children, he would hang around and tell the staff the latest on his ex-wife and choices she was making that he felt were inappropriate for the children. The situation was becoming too much for the staff to deal with, and other parents were beginning to complain about the twins' behaviors.

Communication with both sides of the family was paramount. While sometimes difficult and uncomfortable, beginning conversations with the focus on the children was the director's strategy. In director-organized meetings, the staff talked through their frustration of the twins' mom's choice and their disappointment in her. They also discussed how the dad's conversations were becoming a distraction and prevented them from being able to supervise the class and ongoing daily activities. While sympathetic, the staff felt as if the dad was trying to build support for "his side"—which was both stressful and inappropriate. Both the director and teachers viewed their roles as collaborative. When advocating for the children, each made a commitment to lend support to each other as well as to the twins and the adults in their lives, including Mom, her new boyfriend, and Dad. After these foundational talks to process feelings as well as develop a plan, the director began planning for the next necessary meeting.

Improving Executive Function

At times like these, the director's professional influence and role is key. Initial steps included the director calling each parent separately to acknowledge the difficulty the teachers were having with communication, as well as the children's emotional outbursts. The director communicated to both parents that a meeting—either together or separately—was crucial for addressing the needs of the children. By keeping the focus on the children's needs, the director was able to schedule both parents for the same meeting place and time. Care for the children was arranged and provided by a teacher assistant. The meeting agenda was set to include establishing expectations for communication and boundaries between the parents and with staff, as well as sharing strategies to help the twins manage their strong emotions. On the day of the meeting, Tate and Taylor's parents met with their teacher and the director. While keeping the children's executive functioning in mind, everyone agreed to implement the following strategies:

- Spiral-bound journal: This communication tool was kept in the classroom to foster communication between the parents and all involved in the care of the children. By seeing this exchange between all of the significant adults in their lives, the children observed the importance of **communicating** with words and symbols on paper.

- Management of financial information: Since the stress of the reactions of the adults was a challenge for the children to take on, the program adults created less stress for them. The director put all financial information related to the children's account in two separate envelopes; that way everyone had equal access to information, and this limited the tense communications felt by the teachers and director, and provided developmentally appropriate **control** for the children.

- Picture schedule: This schedule, placed in each child's cubby along with a photo book with pictures of their mom, dad, and other family members, helped facilitate the twins' movement between the parents' homes. The picture schedule showed the classroom routine and activities as well as the routine at home. The parents added or changed pictures of where the twins would be in the evening and what they would be doing. These

visual cues helped **clarify expectations** for the twins and supported their critical thinking.

- Assistance during difficult times (circle time, classroom transitions, and nap): Each child was given small items, such as a squishy ball, Fiddle Focus® for Busy Hands, or other objects during times of upset or distress to help calm and facilitate emotional regulation. The items were small enough for the children to carry with them and use when they felt overwhelmed or were seeking out sensory stimulation. The objects also helped when the group needed to transition. The teachers noticed that when Tate had access to items with different textures, he rubbed these against his face, which helped him calm and regulate his emotions during naptime. The director and teachers allowed Taylor and Tate to take their items home with them. Over time, the items were found to be great transitional objects and supports that helped with consistency in addressing behavior across all environments. In addition, Tate was also moved to a more open space in the classroom away from other children to allow him to manipulate his small object until he drifted off to sleep. All of these strategies supported his **focus** and **self-control**.

- Mad Jar: To combat the twins' angry yelling, they were encouraged to yell into the Mad Jar that the teachers made with their help. Both Taylor and Tate had jars in their cubbies that could be easily accessed when they needed to "get their mad out," as labeled by the teachers initially. After a few times of being coached on how to use the Mad Jar, the twins' took full advantage of the strategy and learned more about **perspective taking**. Initially they used it a lot, but over time their use tapered off as the twins began to regulate their emotions. When they learned of its effectiveness, the parents also implemented a Mad Jar at both homes. They

commented that use varied, but it was a strategy that seemed to help as they worked to calm emotional outbursts at home.

Holistic Program Support

Taylor and Tate needed caring support from their teachers and the director. A key element was the communication between the significant adults in these children's lives. By managing conflict on the tenets discussed in chapter 3, the director managed these circumstances in a very appropriate fashion. She was able to resolve with the staff that conflict was not a negative. Meeting with the twins' parents was necessary and was supported by meeting with the staff members first to process their feelings while also coordinating the agenda for everyone when they finally met together. Once the meeting took place, the approach was one of viewing the resolution to the twins' behaviors as a partnership between everyone by using a safe, comfortable location and ensuring the twins were cared for by a trusted adult. Cooperation was nurtured, which helped everyone maintain control of their emotions, leading to dialogue that was helpful and respectful. Also notable was helping the parents realize that what was taking place was having an impact on the twins. Certain children's books were also recommended to help the parents assist their children in understanding their new lives in two households (see "Children's Books" in the appendix). The director's gentle acknowledgment of the impact on the entire family unit led to collectively determined solutions. While the negative relationships between the adults in the children's life landed squarely on the shoulders of the early childhood program staff, they navigated a difficult situation into one of positive communication and ongoing relationships.

The next two circumstances investigated in this chapter not only required effective communication but also an increased sensitivity to what assistance is needed to support significant loss in a child's life.

Jasmine's and Noah's Disruptive Change: Death of a Parent

Death overall is a difficult topic for anyone at any age. For a child to lose a loved one, especially a parent during their early childhood years, is a trauma with life-long implications and change. Complicating death of a parent with acts of violence only further intensifies the issue. Violence in the lives of many American children across the nation is not just seen on television; it is in our homes, neighborhoods, and schools, and for some, it is an everyday occurrence.

The first child discussed, Jasmine, experienced the devastating results of neighborhood violence. This act of violence impacted the lives of Jasmine and her immediate and extended family, as well as the lives of everyone who had an active role in Jasmine's life. The second child discussed is Noah, who suffered a sudden loss. His father died suddenly from a heart condition at an early age. The trauma of sudden loss in a child's life can mirror the same devastating effects as violence. Many of the strategies discussed in both of these children's circumstances can be used in both situations of sudden loss and violence-induced trauma. Let's turn our initial focus on Jasmine.

Trauma of Violence

Jasmine attended a small, private child care facility in a metropolitan hospital. The facility provided care for the children of the hospital employees and was open twenty-four hours a day to meet the needs of all hospital staff. This made for unique situations and circumstances for the director, James, and his staff. James put in long hours and took great pride in knowing each of the 112 children enrolled in his program. He also took great pride in his low staff turnover, as many of the teachers had been teaching at the center for more than a decade.

Jasmine, now twenty-four months, had attended the center since six weeks of age. Her mother, Angela, and her father, Ben, were both longtime employees of the hospital and worked on different shifts. Jasmine was typically at the center from seven in the morning until seven in the evening. She was in the toddler classroom with Ms. Becky and Ms. Gretchen. Much of the staff worked the same shifts as hospital staff to keep continuity of care and easier scheduling. Jasmine was a typically developing child who had about a seventy-five- to one-hundred-word vocabulary. Ms. Becky reported that Jasmine had always been a very talkative and social baby. She seemed happy to look at books and pictures, point to objects, and interact appropriately with her peers in the classroom.

The director, James, contacted Kari to come to the center to talk to the staff about grief and loss. Jasmine's mother, Angela, died in a convenience store robbery near the hospital on the way home from her night shift. This incident received immediate coverage by the local news station on the morning of the robbery as well as the days following because of the expected tie to local gang activity. James was distraught with the news, as was his staff. Parents were also impacted since many knew the family and were quite fond of Angela. Even seeing Jasmine in the classroom led some of the moms to burst into tears. The teachers expressed concerns about the family and what to do to help them. Initially, Kari helped the staff come up with a plan to help each other during the grieving process. In addition, the hospital coordinated with their grief specialists to assist the parents who were struggling with Angela's violent death. Ms. Becky and Ms. Gretchen were concerned with what to say to her father, Ben, and how to help the family. The staff wanted to do something active to help the family, so they came up with a dinner rotation to make sure Ben and Jasmine had a hot meal. It was important to the staff, especially to Ms. Becky and Ms. Gretchen, to provide this service.

Checking in with James and his staff in the weeks following Angela's death, Kari found that Jasmine had started to act out in the classroom. Becky reported that Ben had been not been bringing Jasmine to child care, but his mother, Lisa, had taken the job of transporting her back and forth. Shortly after the funeral, Lisa, also referred to as "Nana," moved in with Ben and Jasmine and planned to stay long term. Within a short time, the grandmother developed a close relationship with Ms. Becky and reported that she was worried about Ben being depressed. He had withdrawn from her and Jasmine, and rarely left his bed. He was also consumed with following the media coverage of the investigation to find who had murdered Angela. James set up a meeting with Ms. Becky, Ms. Gretchen, the grandmother, Kari, and a social worker available through the hospital. During the meeting, the grandmother expressed concern about Jasmine's behavior. Jasmine was not sleeping at home and was waking frequently and crying for her mom, of which the teachers took note. The staff also encouraged the grandmother to limit any media exposure of Angela's death when Jasmine was in the room. Further, supports were determined to help Ben with his grief. This included a mental health evaluation, which lead to follow-up meetings with him in the home that the social worker and grandmother worked together to schedule and conduct.

In a separate meeting with James and Kari, the teachers discussed their concern with Jasmine's behavior. Jasmine was not sleeping during the regular naptime, she had become very clingy (crying when she was not held), and most notably, she screamed when Ms. Becky left the room. She was not playing with other children or even reading her favorite books. They were also concerned about her lack of speech. She no longer said many words. Instead, she pointed at various objects, cried, or whined. All were behaviors that certainly were not observed until after the death of her mom. Ms. Gretchen also remembered the grandmother's concern expressed in the earlier meeting concerning Jasmine's lack of sleep and bouts of frequent crying for her mom.

Improving Jasmine's Executive Function

Kari worked with Ms. Becky and Ms. Gretchen to come up with a plan to help Jasmine during her time with them. As mentioned in earlier chapters, changes in behavior happen over time and not overnight. Many times, children benefit greatly by having a caregiver who has invested in consistent care and consistent strategies, keeping in mind the importance of a secure attachment that must take place over months of continued care. For Jasmine, it was maintaining consistency in her everyday routines and caregiving activities to support her in having some control over her life. It was confusing and heartbreaking for her and all those who loved her when she would ask for her mom and she wouldn't be there.

Luckily for Jasmine, having a secure attachment to her mother and father meant she was able to form more secure attachments with her caregivers. The grandmother, Ms. Becky, Ms. Gretchen, and the director, James, were able to fill in and meet Jasmine's needs and develop secure attachments. Kari suggested using the framework of Ginsburg and Jablow (2015), and several of the 7 Cs—confidence, connection, coping, and control—were implemented. It was important in this case to recognize that the seeds of resiliency were necessary to support Jasmine:

- Confidence: Jasmine was encouraged to regain confidence when the adults established a very consistent routine at home as well as at the program. This meant that Jasmine's dad had to bring her to school on certain days, and her grandmother went to a local community program to help grieving families with young children, as coordinated by the social worker.

- Connection: It was imperative to maintain consistent connections with Jasmine but amp up the intensity. The team decided that Ms. Becky would be the one to respond to Jasmine's needs and meet them immediately. James added a staff person to the toddler room to help with the workload. Meeting children's needs and demands quickly and without fail has been found to be a necessary tenant of developing secure attachments. Ms. Becky responded to Jasmine every time she cried, said a word, or expressed a desire for something. Although giving this kind of attention was exhausting, Becky began to see a change in Jasmine within a few weeks.

- Coping: Everyone in Jasmine's life was experiencing strong feelings and emotions surrounding the loss of a loved one. Experiencing extreme emotions can be scary for adults and even more so for children. The teachers decided to implement a class-wide activity that fostered learning about different emotions and the beginnings of perspective taking. Ms. Gretchen, who was the creative artist of the two teachers, made pictures of faces with the emotions: sad, happy, excited, and mad. During circle time, she would pull out a face and the children would guess how that face was feeling. As the children grew more aware of the faces and feelings, Ms. Gretchen then began to ask what might make the person feel that way, when had they felt that way, and what would happen if they made someone feel that way.

- Control: Ms. Becky and Ms. Gretchen made room in their daily routine and schedule to allow Jasmine to lead and make decisions that would allow her to feel in control of her life. Jasmine was able to lead the children to the playground, wash her hands without much help from an adult, and make choices about lunch, free play, and outside play.

While Ms. Becky and Ms. Gretchen were implementing these activities during child care hours, Jasmine's grandmother and dad were implementing the same strategies at home. All the people involved in Jasmine's life worked hard to maintain communication about what was working well and what needed more time and tweaking. Consistency across all areas of Jasmine's life was key to fostering the secure attachments that she needed to move forward.

Trauma of Sudden Loss

The second family dealt with loss, but it was not due to violence. Violence provides its own set of trauma and shapes for a lifetime the children and families that experience violence. Sudden loss or death of a loved one is a similar trauma. Noah was a three-year-old in a home child care with five other children. The family child care home was run by Ms. Jenny and her sister, Ms. Lori. Both ladies were taking child development classes at the local college, which is how they met Kari. Jenny had just completed her director's credential, and Lori was working toward her CDA. Noah had received care in the family child care home since he was six weeks old. Ms. Jenny reported that Noah was a very easy baby, and she often worried that she would forget about him because he was so laid back. Noah's parents were actively involved in the programming and activities provided in the home program. Noah's mother, Liz, worked at the elementary school as a teacher's aide, and his father, Gary, worked at an assembly plant in a nearby town. Gary died suddenly one night. Liz awakened to him not breathing and called 911. Noah was awake when the paramedics arrived and started CPR. The neighbor stayed with him while his dad was loaded into an ambulance, and his mom hurried out the door to get to the hospital. Liz called with the news as the neighbor dropped off Noah for Ms. Jenny and Ms. Lori to care for. They too were devastated by the sudden loss and struggled with how to help the family.

A few weeks after this sudden traumatic event, Ms. Jenny called Kari for a consultation about Noah. She was highly concerned about his withdrawn behavior and his lack of interaction, especially language. Where Noah was saying three- or four-word sentences a month ago, he now rarely answered yes and no or requested objects with verbal cues. He had reverted back to pointing and grunting. Lori was concerned about his lack of interaction with his friends in child care. Before, Noah would often wait and watch and then join in with his peers, but he was not even watching his peers play anymore. He had a preferred book and would spend hours flipping pages. He was still hugging and greeting his mom at pickup time, but because of the change in their lives, Liz's friends or family members would pick up Noah, or he would stay with Ms. Jenny and Ms. Lori long after child care hours until mom could pick him up.

One of Kari's suggestions was for Ms. Jenny and Ms. Lori to meet with the mom to come up with a plan to address each concern. It was at this meeting that Liz also shared her concern about Noah's withdrawn behavior. She expressed guilt over having to depend on others to pick him up and felt like she was taking advantage of them when she was late. During this initial meeting, Liz was very open about what she was feeling. Ms. Jenny and Ms. Lori listened to her concerns and reassured her that they were willing to help in any way they could. They came up with a timeline for how long it would take for Liz's schedule to be adjusted and create an end date for the late pickups. Ms. Jenny and Ms. Lori also offered to support Liz in attending a weekly grief group supported by the local church. After this meeting, the focus turned to implementing strategies suggested by Kari in earlier meetings that benefited Noah's daily activity at the family child care home.

Improving Noah's Executive Function

Any trauma in a child's life can wreak havoc on daily schedules and routines. Noah did best when his routine stayed the same. Because of the changes at home and at pickup time at child care, he was having difficulty with all of the disruptions to his life. We've discussed consistency at length throughout several chapters, and it was extremely important to Noah in developing coping skills to deal with change. Noah would shut down and ignore the outside world when he didn't know what to expect or even whom to expect. Most concerning, he was able to shut down so completely, by looking at his book or ignoring everyone, that he was missing out on vital interaction and learning with his peers that would later have an impact on development of executive functioning. All parties involved realized the necessity of developing coping skills as well as providing encouragement and opportunities for peer interaction. Using this framework of need to assist Noah, Ms. Jenny and Ms. Lori implemented the following strategies and activities to support executive function:

- Pickup book: Ms. Jenny, Ms. Lori, and Liz came up with a photo book for Noah to keep in his cubby. The book was printed from pictures Liz had on social media of the friends and family members who helped out the most in their lives. At drop-off every morning, Liz would find the picture of who was going to pick up Noah from child care, and they would mark that page with a laminated bookmark that said "Today." Ms. Jenny and Ms. Lori referred to the pickup book repeatedly throughout the day until Noah would look at it on his own. As time went on, Liz was able to add more bookmarks for future days so Noah could see who was picking him up throughout the week. This seemed to go a long way toward easing stress for Noah. Ms. Jenny reported that after using the book for a few weeks, when Noah would get upset, he would sit in his cubby and flip the pages of his pickup book and ask questions for clarification, which seemed to provide comfort for him and allowed for him to **make connections** at his own pace on who would be caring for him each day.

- Picture play: As the weeks went by, Noah continued to ask for his dad. He would point to pictures of men in books and ask about his dad. Liz kept pictures of Gary around the house, but none were any available at child care. Liz brought a picture of Gary that Noah could keep in his cubby by his pickup book. Initially, Noah would use the picture like he used his book. He would look at it and talk to it and then hang it up in his cubby. One particularly stressful day at nap-time, Ms. Jenny gave Gary's picture to Noah to keep with him while he laid down on his cot. By **taking on this challenge** with the assistance of his teacher, this became part of Noah's everyday routine. He would retrieve the picture, lie down on his cot, and sleep holding the picture. Liz said he was doing the same thing at bedtime every night at home. This strategy allowed Noah to find comfort in the pictures of his dad after he had disappeared from Noah's life so suddenly.

- Peer play: Noah was withdrawn and often ignored his peers. Ms. Jenny and Ms. Lori began slowly encouraging Noah to become **self-directed** and **engaged in learning** by sitting in their laps during circle time, and at a center during free play. They even took the group to the library to support Noah's enjoyment of reading, which included seeking children's books that helped to explain the loss of a parent. Noah did best when he was able to know what was expected of him, how long he was expected to stick with the activity and with whom. Ms. Jenny came up with a simple picture schedule to help him get through what were some of the more uncomfortable activities for Noah. She took pictures of other children sitting in circle time, Noah holding a book or flipping pages for Ms. Lori, and Noah sitting by friends. Ms. Jenny and Noah would go over the pictures together, and then she would set a timer on her phone with how long Noah was expected to engage. When Noah began to have success using the picture schedule and timer, they used these same strategies during center time to help Noah play alongside and eventually with his peers. They made sure to pair Noah up with a higher-energy peer who would take the lead during play. This took the pressure off Noah to come up with ideas on his own and allowed him to observe first, then interact.

As with Jasmine, Noah was also being supported appropriately by his early childhood caregivers, Ms. Jenny and Ms. Lori. They too were providing opportunity for resiliency and growth in his executive functioning. By implementing

opportunities to support his love of books and reading, they were building his confidence to engage. Linking interactions not only with them but also his peers gave him the necessary connection to those involved in his everyday life. This included providing overall supports to the change in his life by coping with an irregular routine that eventually became consistent again. Acknowledging his longing for his dad by providing pictures during stressful times also supported not only his ability to cope but also some control in times when Noah felt that he missed his dad. And, finally, pairing with peers to build opportunities for being with them and doing activity supported opportunities to practice control.

Holistic Program Support

This family child care home worked to provide several of the foundational pillars discussed in chapter 2, specifically, in providing a home that radiated a sense of security by using consistent daily routines by designated adults who supported all of the children in their care. Maintaining ongoing communication with Noah's mom between both providers exhibited a high level of commitment to assisting Liz and Noah while also providing appropriate boundaries. While it's easy to want to swoop in and take over care in this traumatic situation, both Ms. Jenny and Ms. Lori, with outside assistance, were able to come to a place of acceptance of the event and provide ongoing strategies and practices to support Liz and Noah.

More Considerations

Each one of the children in this chapter suffered an acute trauma event that could have led to a significant downturn in each child's development. Jasmine and Noah were progressing developmentally until these disruptive events took place. Great care was taken to make observations that noted the areas that were showing signs of delay, and appropriate activity was planned. Great concern was also shown in regard to primary and secondary attachments for both children since the signs of avoidant attachment were noted. Because of the loss of a parent, Jasmine and Noah needed to feel strong feelings of love and caring between the significant adults in their lives, including the early childhood program staff members.

These real-life events were tolerable stress experiences at the point in time they took place in Jasmine's and Noah's lives. However, should additional stresses continue, the levels could become toxic, which is why an awareness by the program staff would be necessary in the following months and years as they cared for the children and their families. The death of a significant adult in the home has been identified as an adverse childhood experience (ACEs), and these children are considered at risk (Felitti et al. 1998). However, since the early childhood program staff in both instances made referrals to outside resources to include mental health professionals, the significant adults in these children's lives were empowered to strengthen their family structure to limit the impact on the child's overall health and development. This action, once again, supports the research behind the tenets of Strengthening Families by nurturing parental resilience by meeting regularly with all of the significant caregivers in the children's lives; fostering social connections by making referrals to the social worker, mental health professionals, and a local grief support group; furthering an awareness of child development by noticing delays; and providing high-quality classroom environments that recognize the importance of consistency, rituals, and routines (Harper Browne 2014).

While chapter 8 will discuss at length care of oneself, it is important to recognize that the magnitude of these events makes it essential that early childhood professionals take care of themselves and deal with grief and loss in a healthy way. Many times we become attached to the children and families we work with like they were our own. Unfortunately, this places the early childhood professional at risk for emotional and mental health issues. For those family child care home providers who work alone, partnering with another provider in the area or discussion with a family member will be important. Awareness by the director as well as those members of the teaching team in a group environment requires observation and conversations with one another to watch for potential red flags. It is necessary to discuss the stress of caring for children and families affected by death of a loved one.

CHAPTER 6

Natural Disasters and Foster Care

A Fighting Chance for Amal, and Siblings Greyson and Alice

The two life-event stories covered in this chapter describe all-too-common circumstances that many areas across the United States are dealing with. The first is the impact of natural disasters on children's lives. With wild weather patterns, powerful superstorms, and the ever-changing climate, weather disasters are intensifying. These events and other natural disasters, such as earthquakes, tsunamis, and droughts, are terrifying for people of all ages. Though forecasting and monitoring systems try and inform in advance, these disasters are somewhat unexpected. And when they do strike, the 24/7 news coverage tends to play up the drama, which often results in reactions that are not reassuring to children. While these events take time to resolve and are truly never forgotten, they also bring people together to help one another with changes in daily life and routines, displacement issues, and finding a new normal. Survival becomes the priority and, for many, a major miracle in itself.

The second topic will focus on the societal changes that have resulted in large numbers of children experiencing life within state foster care systems. Some of the most recent data provided by the Child Welfare Information Gateway (2014) for 2014 found that there were an estimated 415,129 children in foster care, with 29 percent living in relatives' homes and nearly half, 46 percent, in nonrelative foster family homes. Because of their varying circumstances, these children have case plans that either strive to reunite their families or have them adopted, while others face a life in long-term foster care placements. Any of these options subject these children to changing primary and secondary attachments and force them to experience a multitude of social relationships. And the ramifications of insecure attachment are costly, ultimately having an impact on the child's self-esteem, self-control, and neediness of adults either in a positive or negative way. Unfortunately, for many of the children experiencing life within foster care, it's not uncommon for them to respond to this kind of stress with anger and aggressive behaviors either to themselves or others.

Both scenarios discussed in this chapter are examples of varying trauma. Amal experienced an acute trauma when she and her family survived a weather event that destroyed their home and neighborhood. It was a single trauma at a specific point in her development. Conversely, Greyson and Alice are siblings who have experienced complex trauma. They have been repeatedly removed and placed with a number of foster families and continue to have sporadic visitation with their mother. The trauma they have experienced has occurred over time and consistently. As discussed in chapter 1, acute and complex trauma are different in that they vary by time and event. Though they vary, the outcomes can be similar. Children who experience acute or complex trauma will need intervention, building of protective factors, and building of attachments to caregivers. All of these strategies will help build executive functioning and allow for these children to have more success. Be sure to reference the appendix for the lists of resources to use when issues arise. Let's begin by looking more closely at Amal and her acute trauma event.

Amal's Disruptive Change: Natural Disasters

Amal was a four-year-old living with both parents in a suburb of a metropolitan area. She attended a small child care center during the day while both of her parents worked. A very expressive and social child, Amal had many friends and was involved in activities in the community. On the day of the natural disaster, Amal and her mom went into their storm shelter with other family members. Amal's home and neighborhood were destroyed, along with much of the surrounding community. While not in the direct path of the tornado, the child care center Amal attended also sustained minor damage and had to close for a week for repairs to the roof, cleanup, and the reestablishment of power in the area. Throughout this time, the community was focused on cleanup and helping those who were injured, which was widely covered on local news stations.

Ms. Mya and Ms. Rachel were Amal's teachers. Both talked about how much they enjoyed having her in their class and how she was outgoing and had a bubbly personality. However, after the tornado tore through their community and within a few weeks after the acute traumatic event for Amal, her teachers became concerned about a change in her behavior

They reported that Amal was quiet and fearful, and would cry over things she had not cried over in the past. She would freak out and hide under the sand and water table whenever it rained outside. Loud noises would make her cry, and she would cling to Ms. Mya and Ms. Rachel. To attempt getting out of naptime, she was observed making excuses and displaying inappropriate behaviors. Outbursts of tears took place when the teachers started putting cots down in the room. Ms. Mya noticed that during center time, Amal would play in the dramatic play area and would reenact the tornado with her friends. She would have them hide under the table with pillows until she gave the all clear. Ms. Rachel had noticed that she often drew pictures of tornados during art time, which included drawing her house with a tornado in the sky above it.

When the teachers talked to Amal's parents about their concerns, they also learned of changes at home. Since their home was destroyed, the family had been staying temporarily in an apartment across town from their neighborhood. Both the mom and dad told the teachers that Amal had been having nightmares and waking frequently at night. The family had been very concerned about their housing situation and dealing with federal agencies and insurance companies. Many things had changed in their lives. Moving to an apartment, cleaning up what was left of their home, buying new clothes, toys, and household objects, and living apart from their neighbors and friends was very difficult for everyone.

Improving Executive Function

Ms. Mya suggested to Amal's parents that they talk with the local health department's child development specialist, Ms. Winters. They scheduled an appointment and during that visit agreed for her to come to the facility to help the teachers manage Amal's behaviors. After a few phone calls to coordinate, Ms. Winters spent some time observing in the classroom and then at a separate time met with the teachers and parents to come up with a plan to help Amal and the family through this traumatic event. They decided to implement strategies at home and at the child care center to support Amal's executive function:

- Creating a safe environment: The teachers and parents initially came up with a plan to support Amal's ability to have **focus and self-control** to include feeling safe. Ms. Mya and Ms. Rachel rearranged their classroom and looked closely at their curriculum planning and interactions with the children, using *Preschool Teaching*

Practices by Bloom (2015) as a guide. This assessment tool provided valuable insights, including developing a designated corner of the room called the "safe space." The space had a small couch that had cushy pillows, babies, and soft items to touch. Each family was asked to take pictures of themselves at home. These pictures were laminated and mounted in this area. Books, paper, and crayons were on the shelves next to the area. Calm music was available using a cassette player that the children could turn on and off. Whether this was an opportunity to be alone or with another, the children could be in control of their environment, with reassuring pictures that supported an idea of closeness and "safety" for each child.

‣ While arranging their room, Ms. Mya and Ms. Rachel also intentionally reminded Amal and all of their children that they were safe with them. They talked about how they were safe, how the building was safe, how the teachers would keep them safe, and how their parents would keep them safe. Amal was given the task of drawing out a tornado safety plan for the classroom, which Ms. Rachel wrote out. Both Amal's parents and teachers intentionally reminded Amal frequently that she was safe throughout the day.

■ Validating fears: Every time it rained or Amal heard a sound like thunder, she would immediately start crying, hide under a table, or start to panic. In the beginning, Amal's parents told her that it wasn't a big deal, "just a little rain," and assured her it wasn't a storm. With Ms. Winters's help, the teachers and parents decided that instead of making it not important, everyone should validate Amal's feelings, as they were developmentally appropriate and very real to her after the trauma she experienced. Instead of saying, "It's just a little rain," everyone agreed to validate what was taking place by saying, "I know you are scared. Let's check the weather and make sure it is only rain." By validating Amal's fears and listening to her, the adults helped Amal feel more in control by **communicating** and **making connections** to things happening in her life.

- Helping out: During the cleanup of the community, the child care center and parents decided to collect clothes and personal items for the families who had lost their homes, and bottles of water for the volunteers. This allowed all of the children to participate in an activity that supported **perspective taking**. Amal's family received gift cards from the center to get clothes and other items that were needed. Amal went with her classmates and teachers to visit the local fire department and emergency response center. They delivered water to the firefighters and got a tour of the fire station. During the tour of the emergency response center, Amal had the opportunity to ask questions about the tornado warnings and how emergency response works. All the children were given ideas to help during an emergency as well as what to do and who to call if they ever needed help.

- Recognizing temperament: It was important for the teachers to recognize the varying temperaments of the children in their room to assist with each child's ability to **take on challenges**. Each child processed the feelings and emotions of the tornado according to her temperament based on how she was wired. Talking through or even drawing pictures of the event were found to be helpful for some of the children, while for others it seemed to be disruptive. Ms. Winters provided a parent meeting that helped all of the parents better understand temperament as well as the importance of limiting media exposure. Since local news coverage was constant, it was imperative to support social and emotional recovery and healing at the child and adult level. Parents were reminded to be vigilant when protecting their children and to avoid becoming obsessed with local news coverage.

Holistic Program Support

By using these strategies, Amal was given the opportunity to feel safe, express her own fears, see concrete ways others were helping in the community, and also help out on her own. While adjusting the overall organizational system because of the natural disaster, the team of teachers included a multitude of interactions that emphasized the importance of environments that provided trusting, caring adults who acted as caregivers and role models. When a child suffers an acute trauma, a primary goal of all adults is to remember that the child first needs to feel safe. Providing a safe place may look different in the varying instances of acute trauma, but the bottom line is the same. Children need to feel safe. Once they can rely on the adults caring for them to keep them safe, they are able to access more parts of their brain to create new neural pathways that can alter existing ones—and in this case, the ones that the stress of the tornado created for Amal and her classmates. As discussed in chapter 2, researchers have found that the brain *can* adapt to new experiences, learn new information, and create new memories. With the help of Ms. Winters and a collective effort between Amal's parents and her teachers, Amal and the other children were supported in their healing process.

Greyson and Alice's Disruptive Change: Foster Care

Now that we have learned about Amal and the acute trauma she experienced from a natural disaster event, let's talk about siblings Greyson and Alice. They experienced complex trauma because of frequent placements in foster care. Fortunately, they eventually were placed with Ms. Trish, a foster parent and early childhood teacher. Slowly, they were able to build a connection and subsequently a secure attachment with her. While this was not an easy task, it is important to note that Greyson and Alice were able to do this! Their connection occurred over time and with much hard work by Ms. Trish, her family members, and the early childhood program staff. Along with the successes were many failures, of course, but it was because Ms. Trish put in the work by taking classes and accessing community child development resources that this story has a happy ending.

Greyson, age three, and Alice, age two, were removed from their mother because of extreme neglect and abandonment. Their mother would leave them alone during the night and not return until later the next day. They lived in an apartment that child protective service described as "unlivable." It was apparent to those involved with the case that the children were not fed or were unable to eat regularly. The siblings were removed when Greyson was two and Alice was one. Since being removed from their mother's custody, the children had been placed and removed from five different foster homes. During that time, the children's mother never showed for any court appearances, which led to her being charged with multiple counts of child abuse. Seeing their mom ever again was highly unlikely, and not one family member came forth to claim custody. As a result, the state stepped in and placed the children with Ms. Trish (as both foster parent and teacher), and an intervention and treatment plan was developed and implemented.

Children in foster care often experience complex trauma. Recall that complex trauma is trauma that occurs over time, repeatedly, and can be devastating to the social and emotional health of the children involved. Multiple transitions between family members, foster homes, or group homes set children up to struggle with forming secure attachments, trusting any adults, which then breeds behavior problems and disorders (Child Welfare Information Gateway 2014). This wreaks havoc on children's growing brains and ultimately their executive functioning. As we mentioned earlier, hundreds of thousands of children are living within our nation's foster care system. Because these children experience multiple placements, inconsistent visitation with parents, and a lack of parent and caregiver education, many are experiencing toxic stress events. For children like Greyson and Alice, receiving quality infant and early childhood mental health services, including living in a home with adults who provide protective factors, establishes the best situation to support their challenging behaviors.

Immediately, Ms. Trish noticed that Greyson had the most difficult time adjusting to the multiple foster placements. He was exhibiting aggressive behaviors, hitting and biting, and had a significant speech and language delay. Alice also had developmental delays as the result of neglect and multiple placements. She would hoard food, put food in her cubby at school, take food from her classmates' plates, and overeat until she would get sick. Alice also had few boundaries and little social awareness. She would greet and hug any person who came into the classroom and often would sit on their laps if able. While she had a generally happy disposition, she would cry at transition times if she was not being held. Ms. Trish was most concerned about the global developmental delays of both children and the behavior problems that would become exhausting at the end of the day. At first, Alice was placed in Ms. Trish's classroom with the other children her age. Greyson was placed in the class above Alice because of his age. After a few weeks, the director and Ms. Trish contacted their caseworker, who performed a developmental screening. The results indicated it was best to place Greyson in Ms. Trish's class as well. Although chronologically Greyson was three, his developmental age was two. During the follow-up meeting with the caseworker, it was determined that both children needed to be evaluated by the state's early intervention (EI) program, a federally mandated program designed to meet the needs of infants and toddlers with disabilities and developmental delays.

Improving Executive Function

After the evaluation, the EI team determined that both of the children had significant global delays. Their service plans were developed in conjunction with Ms. Trish and the program staff. Both children needed speech and occupational therapy along with social and emotional services provided by the EI team's social worker. The team provided services at the center as well as at Ms. Trish's house. They suggested strategies for the early childhood program staff to implement as part of the children's treatment plans. The team advised that this was going to be a long process. During the discussion, they advised that it would take time and many tears to progress and reach a point where Ms. Trish, her family, and the program staff would consider it a success. These initial meetings set expectations for all of the adults involved and informed the overall organizational system adjustments that were necessary to support the children. Both Greyson and Alice needed this ongoing support to rebuild and enhance their executive functioning beginning with these strategies:

■ Behavior redirection: Greyson was hurting other children when he wanted a toy or others got too close, or if he was having a bad day. Ms. Trish described Greyson as a "tornado," and it was obvious that he needed help with his **focus and self-control**. He would go into the classroom, or room at home, and destroy it. The team became aware of Greyson's inability to play with toys. He would first throw a toy, then move on to the next toy or center. When Greyson fought over toys, he would bite and pinch. He also did this every time he got in his car seat. He would pinch his sister to the point that she had bruises covering her arms. Decreasing the pinching and biting was Trish's top priority. To help with these behaviors, Greyson was given a six-inch piece of pool noodle. The foamy rubber was inexpensive and easy to carry. When Greyson pinched, he was given the pool noodle and redirected to pinch the noodle. He also was given the noodle when he bit. Ms. Trish noted the times of increased pinching and biting and began giving Greyson his noodle before he engaged with activities during these times. In the car, everyone was given a pool noodle and Greyson was given two, one for each hand. If he threw one or lost one, one was immediately placed in his

hand. His hands were busy with the pool noodles and the pinching stopped. This served as a transition activity for loading up the car as well. Greyson was given the bag of noodles, and it was his job to pass everyone a noodle. Greyson was able to bite off pieces of the noodle, so he was supervised closely when he had one. While this didn't happen often, all of the adults recognized that this could be a choking hazard for smaller children.

- Play: Since Greyson did not know how to play with toys, one of the goals on his treatment plan was to teach him how to play to help him be **self-directed** and experience **engaged learning**. The therapists began with puzzles. Playing with puzzles has a beginning (taking pieces out), a middle (putting pieces back in), and an end (putting the puzzle back on the shelf). The speech-language pathologist chose puzzles with pieces that would elicit speech and language that Greyson was working on. After mastering puzzles alone, he played with puzzles alongside one of his calmer peers. The therapists used a scaffold intervention strategy that supported Greyson in completing the puzzle but allowed him to progress into doing it alone, parallel to a peer, and eventually, along with a peer. Ms. Trish, along with the program staff who observed during these sessions, used these same strategies throughout the day to support Greyson.

- Individual "Busy Bags": These premade items were strategically placed in the classroom for any child who needed a quiet activity during a structured class time. These were little bags with squeeze toys, a velvet color sheet with one marker, a small dry erase board and one marker, a small, slotted office tray with pipe cleaners to loop through slots, or a plastic straw cup with curling ribbon threaded through the straw to then pull through. These were all activities designed to keep little hands busy and support children's **focus and self-control** when a break was needed or when children needed to sit in circle time with the other children. While designed to help Greyson and Alice, these bags were available to all the children, and at first each child wanted one. Once the newness of the bags wore off, the children who needed to use these activities would seek them out, and it was no longer a distraction to others.

- Pretend play: **Making connections** was easier for Greyson when he was outside and able to use large-muscle movements. Ms. Trish would read the book *We're Going on a Bear Hunt* before outside playtime, and then she would lead the children in their own bear hunt outside. In the beginning, Greyson had to be given the things to take with him and modeled in ways to move. He then watched his peers and imitated what they were doing. After some weeks of bear hunting three times a week, he began to come up with pretend objects and movements on his own.

- Social and emotional development: As Greyson was working on curbing unwanted behaviors and learning how to play, Alice was also learning these skills of **taking on challenges** and **communicating**. Alice, along with all the other classmates, participated in the activities and strategies mentioned above. Ms. Trish and the social worker worked hard on establishing an attachment with both children. Ms. Trish and the other teachers at the center were intentional about responding immediately to both Greyson and Alice. Luckily for the children, the teachers were very consistent and loving. They were told multiple times every day that they were safe and loved, and that others were happy to see them. Consistent routines and schedules were most important in the beginning. Ms. Trish adopted a strict schedule and was vigilant that others followed the schedule pictured in her classroom. Greyson and Alice were both given a photo album with pictures of their classmates, teachers, and friends, which stayed with them wherever they went. Ms. Trish would look at the pictures with them before bed every night, and it became a nighttime ritual. New pictures were added by Ms. Trish, and the children chose the photos to go into their album. This was another way to highlight the stability in their lives and reassure them that they would see the same people the next day.

■ Mealtime supports: Alice struggled with mealtimes, which lead to both her and her classmates learning more about **making connections** and **perspective taking**. She would hoard food, take food off other children's plates, and could be very disruptive during mealtime, especially at child care. She exhibited these behaviors at home also. To help with the hoarding of food, Alice was given a part of the meal in a container, often a piece of toast and jelly in a storage bag, to put in the lower part of a cabinet in the classroom. The cabinet was designated for Alice. She put whatever food she was given in a container in her cabinet until the next mealtime or the end of the day. If there was food left over at the end of the day, she would put it in her backpack and take it home to eat there. At first, other children put food in her cabinet until the routine was established. Alice's food cabinet was used every day for the first few weeks. Then she forgot on some days and the behavior tapered off. The cabinet was available to her even after she hadn't used it in a few weeks, because disruption to her routine or any type of change would cause her to hoard food again.

  ‣ During mealtimes, Alice would still take food off others' plates. Ms. Trish did not want to seat her at a table by herself because she didn't want her to be singled out and miss out on opportunities for social interaction. Instead, Ms. Trish sat Alice at the head of the table and scooted her peers farther down, out of arm's reach. She also put her in a chair with a weighted pillow on her lap, then placed a colorful tray holding her food on the pillow. She was able to be with her friends but was provided with visual and pressure cues to keep her seated and to keep her hands on her own plate.

■ Spatial awareness: Alice had very limited spatial and social awareness. She would step on toys when walking across the room, sit on other children during story time, and touch others' work when not appropriate. Helping her with **focus and self-control** while also assisting with her ability to be a **self-directed and engaged learner** was a goal. A member of the EI team brought a mini hula hoop for

Alice to sit in during circle time. Alice had to be reminded frequently to sit in her hoop. Also, an air-filled bathtub headrest pillow was placed inside the hula hoop on the floor for Alice to sit on. The pillow headrest was small enough to be completely covered when sat on, and it was quiet. Alice could wiggle back and forth on the pillow. Further, an individual texture table was used during center time, as Alice had difficulty standing at the classroom's large texture table, and she disrupted other children's play. Ms. Trish gave Alice a large oval plastic serving dish Velcroed to the top of a plastic storage container top. She filled the serving dish with pieces of wrapping paper, scrap paper, cardboard, feathers, safety scissors, and a hole punch. This was a great activity for Alice to work on fine-motor skill development, and it was also helpful in providing a visual and physical boundary. Ms. Trish changed the objects in the classroom texture table frequently and placed the same items in Alice's individual table. Alice especially liked crunching dry macaroni noodles with a garlic press. She responded well to these activities with heavier work and would stay engaged in them longer than in others with less motor movement.

- Children's books: Ms. Trish loved to read to her class and recognized how important it was to support not only Greyson and Alice but all of the children with **making connections** in their learning. The social worker provided a list of children's books (see pp. 125–26) about foster families and moving so Ms. Trish could read them to her class. Alice was often disruptive during reading time, so Ms. Trish gave her the job of book holder. Sometimes Alice would stand and turn pages for Trish; other times she would sit on Trish's lap and hold the book while turning pages.

Holistic Program Support

The success for Greyson and Alice in this early childhood program came initially from a shared vision that Ms. Trish and other program staff members held. While their backgrounds were varied, when they were together within the program walls each day, they supported each other in trying new ideas, addressing each child's individual needs by observing the EI team's skills and using their resources. This staff recognized that these children were not just struggling: they needed a place committed to changing their trajectory so they could one day enter the school system and progress forward in their lives successfully. By acknowledging this, the team was able to provide the warmth, acceptance, and consistency that Greyson and Alice needed. That said, they also recognized that the work with the two children would be stressful. They leaned on one another and communicated frequently between themselves and the outside EI team members. Not only did Greyson and Alice benefit, but all the children were learning to manage frustration, recognize and respond to one another together, and grow cognitively. All these activities were helpful in the early months of placement for Greyson and Alice. As time progressed, they continued to use the intervention ideas and adapted the objects used or modified the activities to meet Greyson's and Alice's developing needs. After weeks of successful mealtimes and decreased behavior problems and food hoarding, there would be a bad day where these behaviors would come roaring back, and the teachers and therapists would have to implement the intervention strategies. Patience, understanding, and commitment were key to supporting Greyson and Alice.

More Considerations

Events shared within this chapter were examples of acute, complex, and chronic stress events. While Amal needed her security reestablished, Greyson and Alice never had security in the first place. Notice that connection to significant adults and peers was a common thread for all of these children, and their play was supported by creating environments that had props and specific play interactions to steer inappropriate behaviors into appropriate ones. While Amal could draw strength from the relationships with the adults in her life, Greyson and Alice needed to build those relationships with a group of adults fully committed to becoming a rock of support through good times and bad. Notice that while both events were very stressful, Amal experienced a tolerable stress event, yet Greyson and Alice were dealing with high levels of toxic stress, causing erratic behaviors that were very difficult to manage. Both teams of early childhood professionals embraced these children and made necessary organizational system adjustments to allow them to learn and grow, and to develop their executive functioning.

Most important when reflecting on the ACEs study is the high risk that both Greyson and Alice had, even if their young ages meant they weren't conscious of all they were exposed to. By Ms. Trish and the early childhood staff seeking out early intervention and embracing these children in their lives, they hoped to mitigate some of those adverse experiences and change Greyson's and Alice's trajectories. They became the "toxic-stress busters" to strengthen and provide a family unit for Greyson and Alice. Amal and her classmates as well as Greyson and Alice were given the supports of resiliency. The adults throughout these experiences created opportunities for the children to feel confident, experience positive connections, create appropriate ways to cope, and have control in their lives. Overall, each family experienced a staff that communicated appropriately, nurtured parent resilience, fostered social connections by using professional services, and created high-quality classroom activities and environments that surrounded a bedrock of consistency.

Children with a Medical Diagnosis

A Fighting Chance for Abe and Zoe

A s first detailed in an article written for *Child Care Exchange* (Humphries and Rains 2012), Dr. Jane and Kari provided insight into the changing life for Abe and his family. The teachers who cared for him as an infant were the first to make troublesome observations. As Abe grew, his parents had to come to a place of acceptance and seek resources. The roller coaster of feelings, thoughts of inadequacy, and overall confusion as to what might be taking place was difficult for the significant adults in Abe's life.

This chapter goes on to explore Zoe's experiences as the sibling of a child with a complex medical diagnosis. Zoe's issues, while not due to her own health, were complicated by the needs of a brother who took up everyone's time and energy. Between care at home, multiple doctor visits, and treatments that her brother had to receive to stay well, Zoe suffered from her parents' unintended neglect in meeting her social and emotional needs. Once again, these real-life stories capture how the director and teachers were the consistent and caring place where these children had understanding and stability. These final two stories are of children and families going through two major scenarios of medically related disruptive change that will once again share practical strategies and ideas of how early childhood program staff managed and supported these children's lives. Be sure to reference the appendix for the lists of resources to use when issues arise.

Abe's Disruptive Change: Medically Diagnosed Child

When Abe joined the program as an infant, the teachers in the classroom began to notice issues that made caring for Abe just a little more sensitive. As Abe grew into a mobile toddler, he would cover his ears when classroom noise got loud, cry when other children touched him, and often hide under tables to get away. The staff wanted to meet Abe's individual needs, but they felt inadequate. The teachers knew of early intervention services by the state and encouraged Abe's parents to seek these services. At first, Abe's parents were very upset by the staff's request, which created tears and frustration on both sides. Denial and grief that their child was not "normal" affected Abe's parents—feelings not uncommon among parents in the same circumstances. Luckily for Abe, the staff and director were patient and empathetic, and they listened. After multiple assessments and meetings with Abe's parents and center staff, Abe was diagnosed with sensory integration issues and work began to include several qualified specialists in his care.

Initially, Abe received services in the home environment. Over time, the director began to observe the teachers become increasingly anxious about how to meet Abe's needs while also caring for the other children in the classroom. A couple of the teachers mentioned at a staff meeting that they weren't ready to handle Abe, and the thought of his joining their classroom in the fall was creating stress for them. Abe was not the only child in the group who needed attention, and as he got older and bigger, managing his behavior in conjunction with the behavior of some of the other children in the group was increasingly overwhelming. Abe's parents could sense the teachers' apprehension. Fortunately for Abe, his family, and his teachers, the state's early intervention program provided training and expertise within the center environment. The director, who was central to the ongoing coordination effort, found herself playing a significant role in determining how best to serve Abe and his family while also supporting the other children in the classroom as well as the staff. Let's take a closer look at this director and staff's journey.

Over the past several years, early childhood professionals have had a multitude of different diagnoses brought to their attention. While diagnoses vary, parents and adult family members all expect their child's needs will be met. But these expectations for individual children can sometimes become difficult to meet because of a lack of funds and staff expertise in certain areas. In Abe's case, it was important that the director and staff have a better understanding of sensory integration issues in young children. While researching and talking with professionals, Abe's teachers found that children with sensory processing problems may present very similar behaviors as a child who is diagnosed with attention-deficit/hyperactivity disorder (ADHD), such as having difficulty focusing on tasks, modulating their desire to touch objects and people, and engaging in constant movement and excessive talking. While the behaviors may look similar, the outcomes can vary greatly. These same behaviors can lead to a misdiagnosis of ADHD if they are not addressed appropriately. In Abe's case, his parents and teachers sought out and worked with professionals in the community who provided a correct diagnosis and treatment plan suited for home and for the early childhood program environment.

While a diagnosis of sensory integration dysfunction can be complex, here are some of the basic ideas that surround it (Ostovar 2009):

- Sensory integration is a neurological process.

- The brain gathers sensory information from the environment and then organizes that information to help our bodies respond.

- We use our senses to learn about what is going on around us and to interact appropriately in our environment. Through touch, hearing, taste, sight, smell, movement, and balance, we learn, interact, and organize the sensory information around us.

- We process the sensory information in our world simultaneously.

- When the sensory integration system is intact, the child is freely able to learn. When the child has difficulty in this area, it interferes with learning.

For Abe during circle time, he sees the teacher and other children, feels the carpet square beneath his legs, hears other children playing outside, and smells the paint from an earlier art activity. His brain (and those of children with similar issues) is constantly taking in information from all five senses and organizing and then responding to that information. When the brain, or central nervous system, is unable to process this information correctly, a sensory processing problem can occur. Abe, as a child with a sensory processing problem, may have difficulty sitting in circle time. A sensory processing problem with touch makes sitting on a carpet square feel like sitting on sandpaper. As a result, Abe may not be able to sit for any length of time and will have trouble attending to the group activity.

Abe's teachers were helped by the early intervention team's explanation of the differences on the diagnostic spectrum. Abe tended to display sensory-avoiding behaviors. However, other children on this diagnostic spectrum may display sensory-seeking behaviors. Children within the sensory processing disorder diagnostic category may respond to sensory input with a wide spectrum of responses, ranging from overresponsive to underresponsive, sensory-seeking to sensory-defensive (Dunn 1997). Seeking more information from professionals when sensory processing dysfunction is suspected is vital. The strategies, activities, and interventions may be significantly different when dealing with sensory-avoiding behaviors as opposed to sensory-seeking behaviors.

Improving Executive Function

Becoming a champion for all the children in the classroom was the direction that both the director and Abe's teachers embraced. Abe's teachers learned flexibility and recognized that there were no cookie-cutter approaches when working with him and the other children exhibiting challenging behavior in the classroom. Strategies and activities that were developed and implemented also supported Abe and his classmates' executive function:

- Help children accept one another's needs: The children wore laminated badges of interesting shapes and colors to show when they wanted others to know how they were feeling. These included red badges in the shape of a stop sign that said "Stop! No touching today, just words!" This activity supported **communicating** by Abe and between him and his classmates.

- Model actions and words: For example, when a child went over and grabbed Abe's arm, he forcibly withdrew his arm and began to scream at the unannounced, unexpected touch. The teacher said, "Abe doesn't want your help. I'll play with you or help you find something else to do." Abe and the other children were learning **perspective taking**.

- Set up environments that best support children: This strategy was as simple as turning off the music during free play and providing headphones or earbuds for short periods of time when planning any loud activity. Abe was also offered a "cool-off tent" or special cubby he could sit in when he needed to get away. This allowed Abe to **take on challenges** based on recognizing his needs.

- Make naptime adjustments: Naptime was always difficult for Abe, so he was given access to fidget toys, including squishy balls, dog and cat toys with textures, Silly Putty, handheld water and maze games, and books. His cot was placed away from music and windows, and heavier blankets helped keep Abe on his cot. These strategies provided more opportunities for Abe to be supported in **taking on challenges** to meet his needs related to naptime.

- Change circle time materials and equipment: Beanbag chairs (versus carpet squares) were found to be more effective. Abe and the other children with challenging behavior were seated on the outer edges of the circle or in teachers' laps and were being supported in **self-directed, engaged learning** opportunities.

- Establish physical boundaries: Teachers used big boxes filled with a variety of items, such as packing peanuts, beans, and blankets, to help children learn about their bodies in space and to develop spatial awareness. The children also used wet chunky chalk to outline their bodies during outside play. Blanket rides, for Abe and others, were a very successful body play. A child sat on a heavy blanket or comforter and another child pulled the blanket with the child on it. For the older children, an obstacle course was added. Children were being engaged not only with **perspective taking** but also **critical thinking** to support one another.

- Use cues for transitions: An egg timer was used to help pace cleanup time. In addition, posted schedules with movable pictures provided visual prompts for the children to follow. Additional visual cues, such as turning off the lights to signal a break in activity, were also used with Abe and the other children, serving as opportunities to **focus** and learn **self-control**.

- Anticipate difficult situations: In larger groups, placing Abe and other children with challenging behavior at the front or end of the line helped to avoid chaotic or "too touchy" situations—yet another **focus** and **self-control** strategy.

- Institute new practices: Giving children jobs to perform, such as carrying the clipboard, holding the toy bucket, sweeping, wiping off the tables, holding the teacher's hand, and wearing weighted backpacks throughout the day, provided an anchor and sense of security while also supporting **perspective taking**.

- Provide manipulatives: Provide a variety of textured items, such as a Fiddle Focus® for Busy Hands, soft stuffed animals, or a burlap cloth during musical activities to hold and manipulate. These items extend children's **focus and self-control** and also helped Abe to transition to activities and keep his interest during center activities.

Holistic Program Support

The journey of this director and staff began with a commitment to Abe and his parents. By learning more about sensory integration, everyone began to understand that changes to the environment and flexibility were necessary:

- They learned that what worked one day might not work the next.

- The director supported the staff by recognizing that supporting children with sensory integration issues required lots of energy.

- They tapped into state-supported intervention programs and other resources.

- The teachers, mindful of children's different sensory needs, guided their play so children with complementary sensory systems were able to play together while teachers were also learning to adapt to Abe's needs.

- They provided a carefully balanced adaptation to the classroom structures and a focus on multiple activities and strategies within the classroom environment to help Abe and his classmates.

When diagnosed with sensory processing problems, children like Abe begin their academic careers in the early childhood program. Planting the seeds of success in early childhood settings will help these children and families as they continue their journey into other educational environments. The sensory strategies, adaptations, and activities children learn today will have a considerable impact in the future. As this director and teachers found in their journey with Abe, their commitment began with him, the other children, and all families served in their program. Further, a willingness to seek out resources and assistance, adapt and embrace change in the classroom, and extend their professional learning and growth were all necessary ingredients for a successful classroom and support for Abe.

Zoe's Disruptive Change: Sibling of a Medically Diagnosed Child

The diagnosis of disorders and diseases in children has increased in number and accuracy in recent decades. While children are typically not referred for testing until school age, they are evaluated at the first signs of problems. Those working in early childhood classrooms are on the front lines and must be able to recognize the early warning signs of many developmental delays and disorders. That said, remember that those in early childhood classrooms should refer children who display warning signs to appropriate professionals and support that process—not diagnose. It is sometimes easy to use knowledge and experience gained working with children with a specific diagnosis and apply it to others with some similar characteristics. Be careful when drawing conclusions about disorders in young children. Many of the issues that children have share characteristics with other diagnoses that only professionals can distinguish. But what about those children who have a sibling or a parent struggling with a significant medical diagnosis? They have their own warning signs and issues that must be tended to, which brings us to the story of Zoe and her brother Braden.

Zoe was a kindergartner in Mrs. Brown's class, which was an all-day program at the local public school. New to the community, Zoe and her brother had been at the public school for only a short amount of time, because Braden had been expelled from two other schools in surrounding communities. Braden was eight years old and in second grade. The teachers for both children and the principal, Mr. Capps, met with Zoe and Braden's parents prior to enrollment. Their parents were very open and honest with their concerns and Braden's recent diagnosis. Three months prior to the meeting, he had been diagnosed by a developmental pediatrician as having bipolar disorder. His parents were still adjusting to the diagnosis and what that meant for their family. Braden was in treatment with a child psychologist twice a week and had just begun a new medicine to help with mood swings and violent outbursts. The teachers and Mr. Capps listened to the parents' concerns. They reassured the family that they were welcome at their school, and they wanted to provide a safe place where the children could grow and develop. They eased the parents' anxiety by assuring them they would do everything they could to avoid Braden being expelled.

After a few weeks into the new school year, Braden seemed to be leveling off, but Zoe was not acting like what Mrs. Brown had come to know as her typical self. She was more irritable, would disengage from group activities, chose to be by herself in various activity areas within the room, and refuse to leave physical education activities, and she would become agitated and start crying when it was time to do classwork. After observations by Mr. Capps to assist Mrs. Brown in collecting pertinent information, they both decided to talk to her parents about Zoe's behavior. Her parents reported that although Braden was doing well at school, he was struggling at home. He had begun to have long tantrums nightly, staying awake all night, and had even punched a hole in his bedroom wall the previous night. Zoe's parents had not noticed any unusual behavior in Zoe, but they admitted that all of their attention and energy had been focused on Braden. This meeting was a key moment in the relationship building between the parents and the school teacher and principal. Her parents admitted to feeling guilty about the amount of time Braden took and felt that Zoe was loved but often overlooked. Mr. Capps and Mrs. Brown reassured her parents that they were not being judged, listened to their worries, and helped them think of ways to help the family during this extremely stressful time, as well as obtained their permission to use their school counselor as a resource.

Improving Executive Function

Mrs. Brown met with Mr. Capps and the school counselor after the meeting with Zoe's parents. It was decided that Mrs. Brown should increase her interactions and provide intentional activities with Zoe during the time she was in school. By spending more structured time with her one-on-one, they hoped to alleviate some of the behavior issues Zoe was exhibiting. They also determined that a balance of structured involvement with peers would assist with supporting not just her social and emotional development but also her executive functioning as she continued to become a part of their learning community in the classroom. The following are several activities and strategies that were determined and implemented:

- Targeted attention: Zoe and all the other children in the classroom were always greeted by Mrs. Brown. When Zoe arrived, the counselor would assist Mrs. Brown so she could be available to spend time with Zoe. She helped her get her stuff in her cubby and let her choose between two previously designated activities—puzzles or snap beads, playdough or a book, and other activities that Zoe had expressed interest in. The teacher sat with Zoe while she completed her chosen activity. During this time, the teacher commented about what she was doing, describing what the activity was, and never asked questions. This provided a reduced stress time where Zoe was able to play and spend time with an adult who would not ask her questions but rather allow Zoe to take the lead in the conversation by simply listening and watching. It was through this activity that Zoe was **making connections** and **communicating**, while also setting up her day in a positive way.

- Helper roles: One of Zoe's strengths was her great desire to help! Mrs. Brown steered this in a positive direction, which included her working with peers by **taking on challenges** to complete tasks. This included having available a spray bottle with a little water and assorted sponges (with handles) and small dustpan  with handheld brush for any special cleanup issues that Mrs. Brown noticed needed attention in the classroom. Whether it was wiping tables, windows, walls, shelves, or other items in the class, this motor activity was simple, engaging, and could be done alone or with a peer. This helped Zoe and the children to continue caring for their classroom and build a sense of community.

- Roll of the dice: One situation in which Zoe seemed to fall apart was when it was time to do structured classroom activity. To help support her ability to **focus** and gain **self-control**, Mrs. Brown used

a couple of large foam dice that Zoe could roll to obtain a number that would then give her some control over how long she would work on the assignment before taking a break, how many pages she needed to read before taking a break, or how many math problems she needed to complete. The possibilities were endless to how the roll of the dice was used to help Zoe, which even included use during transition times from the gym back into the classroom. When she was not ready to leave the gym class, the roll of the dice determined how many more times Zoe could jump with the jump rope, run laps around the gym, or blow on a provided pinwheel before returning to her class.

- Individual texture support: As mentioned earlier, Zoe struggled with settling in at her place at the table to do classroom work. Her parents purchased a Fiddle Focus® for Busy Fingers that was Velcroed to her place at the table. This item, with its variety of cloth textures and "push" feel, helped her to scratch, rub, and push while  fiddling to **focus** and learn **self-control**. As an added opportunity, Zoe's parents purchased a lap desk so Zoe had an additional option to do her work on. Holding the desk in her lap offered appropriate pressure on the tops of her legs, and the Fiddle Focus® for Busy Fingers could be moved to the lap desk to provide individual texture support to assist her in completing classwork.

- Special project bag: While Zoe and her classmates were involved in projects that supported their critical thinking throughout the day, Mrs. Brown would put special project choices in smaller containers and place them in a bag for the children to take turns picking out as a "surprise" focus (similar to the Get It Back Together Bag). For example, to support science learning in the fall, one of Zoe's classmates chose from the bag an opportunity to make a class leaf mural. The children sat with the teacher and planned what day of the week they would go out together to pick up leaves off the playground, how the leaves would be handled, where they would be stored, and then how they would categorize the leaves and put the mural together. This reflected a commitment by Mrs. Brown to engage the children's minds in **problem solving** by sequencing, trying new processes, evaluating those processes, and seeing results and thinking about them as a result of the engaged activity it created.

■ Addressing fears: Within a few weeks after the meeting between Zoe's parents and teachers, Braden had trouble adjusting to his new medicine and was placed in the hospital. The parents talked with Mr. Capps, the school counselor, and Mrs. Brown about Braden's absence, as they knew prior to his leaving. Zoe was told that her brother was sick and going to a special hospital to get better and that he would come back home. Zoe was distraught the day after Braden left for treatment. She was very clingy to Mrs. Brown and wanted to climb in her lap during circle time as well as at other times throughout the day. In the days after Braden left, Zoe was encouraged to color pictures for her brother. They also read books about children who go to the hospital and found a book about bipolar disorder titled *Eli the Bipolar Bear*. The other children were curious about where Braden had gone and why Zoe was so sad. To address this curiosity and perspective-taking opportunity, Mrs. Brown and the counselor discussed what to talk about and how much information to give the children with the therapist who had been treating Braden. During one circle time, the children were encouraged to ask questions about Braden. The adults addressed each of them, sticking to answering the specific question and not elaborating too much. The questions were mostly about where he was staying, who was with him, what he ate, and what care he was receiving. The children also asked about the diagnosis and if it was contagious and if he would die. After this question-and-answer time, the children, including Zoe, all drew pictures for Braden. His parents took the pictures to Braden on their weekend visit. The teachers also had the children, as a group, make a list of things they would do with Braden when he returned. This helped all of them by assuring them that he would be coming back and by teaching a powerful lesson related to **perspective taking**.

Holistic Program Support

While Zoe was not the diagnosed child, the result was still a disruption for her life. This included unintended neglect at home and constant change and upheaval that extended into her school environments because of her brother's behaviors.

Because of the interest and concern shown by the school staff, Zoe was able to receive a balance of social and emotional supports to continue her cognitive growth in the classroom setting. Rather than being drawn into the children's past, the school personnel approached the situation with the issues at hand and continued to move forward to best help the family cope and regain confidence not only in their family structure but also in functioning in school life.

More Considerations

In this final chapter, we looked at great examples of how these program staff members worked to create positive foundations in their classroom arrangement and management. As noted in chapter 2, opportunities for sensory play, explorations, discovery, and experiences with a range of materials and people are important in the healthy development of children. Both classroom environments used observations of not only the children in question but of all the children within the classroom space. Adjustments were made to elements of the curriculum and activities, while paying close attention to individual abilities and circumstances. All of the strategies and opportunities were matched to each child's needs and/or scaffolded to support the child's learning at different levels.

In noting these individual differences, the teachers in Abe's classroom as well as in Zoe's provided clear and consistent responses and encouraged peer relationships. Strategies for support included developmentally appropriate activities, pairing with peers, and the establishment of and constant communication between all significant adults in the child's life. Zoe, in particular, experienced consistent, patient, tolerant, and caring interactions, even though she was not the one with the diagnosis. While her actions were out of control, these behaviors were managed with loving acceptance and kind intentions not only by the adults but also by the other children in the classroom community. Both of these children, traumatized by their circumstances, received support to thrive in environments where they experienced calm and caring interactions with adults—those who nurtured and connected to them.

CHAPTER 8

Change over Time and Care of Oneself

Throughout the previous chapters, we investigated scenarios of children with significant disruptive events in their lives. The children experienced program environments that offered respite and support, strengthened their emotional resources, and responded to their trauma so they were able and ready to learn. Gracie, a child whose family experienced homelessness, had teachers who worried daily about her welfare: Will she have a safe place to eat tonight, food to eat, or enough attention and love from her parents overwhelmed by trying to reestablish a home life? While Quinton had grandparents who offered extraordinary support, each day his teachers saw the worry and anxiety on his face and in his actions due to the poor choices of his dad and mom.

In chapter 5, we explored children desperate to connect with those who were floating in and out of their parents' multiple relationships, and Jasmine's and Noah's sudden loss of a parent. Jasmine and Noah felt the heartbreak of losing the parent connection under tragic circumstances, and the teachers witnessed daily the resulting sadness and anger felt by these children. As we saw in chapter 6, the teachers supporting Amal and her classmates after the tornado ripped through their community not only endured the day of the event but also had to watch continual news coverage and drive through the devastated areas only to be reminded of the loss in their community. They continued to work daily with anxious children who when storm clouds approached became agitated and even more stressed.

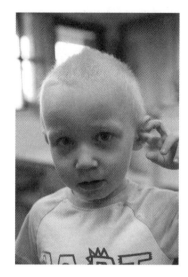

In Greyson's and Alice's stories, we saw how the program environments were the only constant in their lives as they endured multiple placements in homes while navigating their state's foster care system. Finally, we examined the impact of medical diagnosis for Abe, who was sensory sensitive, as well as for Zoe, who had to sort through the daily complexities of having a brother with a significant medical diagnosis. *None* of the children asked for the complexity that these disruptive events afforded them, yet they were forced to cope and learn resilience—which is also important for the adults working with them.

Anyone working with children experiencing disruptive change will at times feel hopeless and helpless. The types of issues and the level of their intensity can create situations where early childhood professionals feel they have failed. Few have expertise in dealing with frequent crises and high incidences of trauma. While many higher education programs along with a variety of resources published recently have been striving to meet this need, the field is still underprepared in this area. For many choosing a career in early childhood, the main focus has always been about embracing children's wonder and excitement, while providing environments that are safe, healthy, and secure. The goal is to teach children through play, interactions, and relationships and to set forth a trajectory for success. That said, no matter what education level an adult brings to the program environment, it is certain that at one time or another administrators, teachers, program staff, and family child care home providers will have to deal with children who are experiencing incredible stress due to life events that are out of their control. In this final chapter, we want to address one topic we haven't really covered yet: the need for program staff to care for themselves before, during, and after the change in the lives of the children in their care. We will also provide a framework of support within the program environment.

An Adult Awareness

As discussed in chapter 1, strong early childhood programs are the crucial connection to relationships and the key to giving children exposed to these traumatic events a fighting chance. These environments nurture hope and strength not only for the child but also for the child's parent or significant caregiver. At one end of the spectrum, the work is intense, tedious, frustrating, challenging, and stressful. On the other end, this work can also provide a sense of accomplishment and reward when supporting these children.

The key to being successful is learning and understanding the perspective of what is taking place in the child's life and then adjusting *yourself and the approach to respond to the child* accordingly. To do this, you must learn how to manage your own shock and response to events. Feeling underprepared, overwhelmed, frightened, or helpless is not uncommon. As discussed in the introduction, the events of April 19, 1995, were terrifying for Dr. Jane and her staff members. This human-made disaster was hard to believe in the minutes and hours that followed. But after days and weeks passed by and officials began to piece together why the bombing happened, knowing that children—little boys and girls—and those who had cared for them were a target was heartbreaking. The reality was that early childhood programs were vulnerable, and the bombing forced Dr. Jane and her program staff to think about safety and security from a totally different lens—a lens that included thinking about an emergency and evacuation plan and verifying the identity of everyone who entered the building. Immediate changes had to take place in everyday operations so that a sense of security was evident to the parents, children, and staff members. While there was no disaster framework exclusive to early childhood at that time, over the years and after many events and circumstances, many resources are now available to include plan expectations as set forth in state and federal requirements. These plans have also included information surrounding the issue of media coverage.

As we discussed in chapter 6, the media exposure of natural or human-made events have provided extraordinary images and stories. While we've talked about how these have an impact on children, we must stress that adults are affected as well. Early childhood professionals have to lessen their media exposure and stay vigilant to avoid conversations in front of children. Although tempting, watching live or continual coverage of the event should be avoided. Furthermore, staff members should keep in mind these behavioral warning signs after natural or human-made events:

- displaying strong emotions, such as sadness, anger, fear, guilt, shock, moodiness, and helplessness

- feeling disconnected, hopeless, or numb to others' needs

- a strong need to be either alone or with someone at all times

- lack of appetite or overeating

- sleep-related issues, including restless sleep or fatigue

- arguing with coworkers and other adults

- irritability

- survivor's guilt

- decreased intimacy

- general and unexplained aches and pains, headaches, or stomach issues

- trouble focusing or concentrating

- increase in alcohol consumption and/or substance abuse

Should you notice any of these warning signs in yourself or your coworkers, accessing the appropriate resources is important and a responsibility that all staff members have to one another. For those working in isolation, having a family member or friend who serves as this sounding board is an important element to consider. This way, when tackling the daily work with fragile children and families, they too have an outlet to have their own professional needs met. As one director of a homeless shelter that provided child care services shared with Dr. Jane and Kari, "I tell my staff, if you are not talking to me—I get worried about you. The work we do is taxing, socially and emotionally." Her approach to the importance of discussion supports the need for reflective supervision, a technique that many programs are incorporating into their support systems for staff.

Considering reflective supervision as a foundational element for infant and early childhood programs is important (Eggbeer, Mann, and Seibel 2007). With the tremendous weight that this work can create, early childhood professionals can become isolated and burn out very quickly if they cannot communicate their feelings in safe relationships. This typically can be mitigated by a supervisor and an employee when both participants engage in active listening and thoughtful questioning. It is best if this takes place on a regular schedule and is done either individually or in groups and by supervisors or peers (Gilkerson and Shahmoon-Shanok 2000). While not therapy, reflective practice is about supporting individuals to think about their daily interactions and in an honest and trustful environment, analyze what took place, and then make adjustments in their daily practices with children. This opportunity allows an individual to learn one's strengths and weaknesses in a safe conversation, which then enhances the person's learning and practice. Since working with complex family situations is difficult, individuals who are with the children each day *need* opportunities to ultimately foster their well-being. This is crucial to having staff members that are effective when in the program environment. Following are tips and recommendations for how to create those opportunities for well-being (Donahue, Falk, and Provet 2000):

- Find a balance of empathy to avoid being overwhelmed by the trauma that is taking place.

- Avoid falling into the trap of believing that showing any sign of weakness could be a sign of being unprofessional—recognize that these events will stir up feelings.

- Acknowledge that sometimes it may feel easier to just ignore what is taking place; however, if that happens, this may be putting the family and child more at risk by not seeking out appropriate interventions.

- Allow staff opportunities to participate in formal support groups to talk through frustrations and stress.

- Offer opportunities for meetings where staff can share traumatic events that resonate with them.

- Remind yourself that sometimes what is taking place in the child's life is uncontrollable.

Today there are more children who have several traumatic issues taking place simultaneously, and early childhood professionals must be aware and informed. Forty-six percent of children in the United States have experienced at least one event from the ACEs study (Sacks, Murphey, and Moore 2014). Staying current about the topics of domestic violence, alcohol or drug abuse, mental illness, exposure to neighborhood violence, homelessness, and the impacts of foster care

on young children is imperative. When children witness or become part of those events, they can display behaviors that become very intense and erratic. Relationships with the family members of these children can become frayed and cause tension between families and staff and program members. These experiences may lead to more severe difficulties and challenges over a longer time. Not surprisingly, many working in early childhood programs become frustrated and stressed because of the intense needs and care these children must have, which sometimes includes the baggage of adults who are acting out.

That said, many fields, including medical services, counseling, social work, and case management, have to deal with difficult and hard-to-reach families. Familiarizing yourself with local resources and knowing how to access them—such as consultations with early childhood mental health professionals who work within program environments—can make a difference in steering these families toward a path of stability.

While many school systems and Head Start programs have service structures in place with coordinating staff, many early childhood programs do not have this opportunity. A constant awareness of what community resources are available for families of all income levels must be a priority for program staff—not just the director (see pp. 119–121). Many times it is the collective awareness and thinking by the group that lend insight to next steps for families. Parents and other adult family members view their child's teacher as an expert and expect the teacher to know these facts as well as provide them with credible information. This also extends to referrals for staff members who are struggling with the day-to-day pressures of work and home life.

Stress in life is a reality for adults just as it is for children, but adults have had a little more practice in learning how to cope with it. As noted in chapter 1, adults who choose to work with young children could also have had adverse childhood experiences themselves. Because of this, their sensitivity will be much more heightened and could be triggered a bit more quickly. It may be best to take time to understand the ACEs study score by asking the following (Felitti et al. 1998): Based on your own experiences as a child, how many of these statements would be answered "yes"?

1. A family income that was or has been very hard to get by on; for example, it was hard to cover the basics like food or a place to live

2. A parent or guardian who got divorced and/or separated

3. A parent or guardian who died

4. A parent or guardian who served time in jail or prison

5. Witnessed parents, guardians, or any other adults in the home being slapped, hit, kicked, or punched, or who beat each other up

6. Was the victim of physical, emotional, and/or sexual abuse

7. Lived with someone who was mentally ill, suicidal, or severely depressed for more than a couple of weeks

8. Lived with someone who had a problem with alcohol or drugs

Give one point for each "yes." A score of four or more places a person at a higher risk for a variety of health and social problems:

- suicide attempts

- fetal death

- unintended pregnancies

- depression

- health-related quality of life

- chronic obstructive pulmonary disease

- heart disease

- liver disease

- HIV/sexually transmitted diseases (STDs)

- adolescent pregnancy

- smoking

- alcohol and substance abuse

The health implications of this list are staggering. For those working with children and families each day, an awareness of individual ACEs scores helps all the adults become more aware and to work toward providing safe, stable, and nurturing relationships and environments that everyone can benefit from—including personal health. As leaders and teachers in early childhood programs, we must recognize what each of us *can* do as an individual when supporting those team members who are struggling with ongoing stress:

- Respect the person's need for privacy and private grief.

- Reassure the person that he or she is safe.

- Maintain a personal presence with the person.

- Encourage laughter and play in daily life.

- Voice support with assistance and sympathy.

- Listen and empathize, and talk only when necessary.

- Offer support to find and access resources.

- Encourage physical exercise to relieve stress and offer to do it together, including deep breaths to help calm.

- Provide as well as encourage well-balanced meals and snacks and adequate rest.

- Discourage making big life changes or decisions.

- Encourage yoga and meditation.

Keeping stress manageable in a typical program environment is a challenge. Add several children experiencing disruptive change in their lives, and this creates even more noise and more opportunities for tension between staff and parents.

However, know that it's possible to juggle all the responsibilities when supported by excellent program leadership, and program support often results in nurturing and productive environments for all children.

Holistic Program Support

As noted in earlier chapter discussions on formulating a collective program vision, Margie Carter and Deb Curtis (2010) encouraged a vision that supported warmth, acceptance, consistency, manageable stress, security, respect, and commitment to one another. With this in mind, this section sets forth practical considerations to support that overall vision. And a crucial part of this vision are those who, like you, are determined to embrace and serve challenging children and their families. Vulnerability is a certainty when working with high-risk families, so it will be important to have well-developed policies to help protect staff from the ongoing drama that these families tend to bring to the program environment. For example, as discussed in chapter 5, the twins' parents were intentionally putting the teachers and director in the middle. But, as the saying goes, sometimes the best defense is a good offense. Consider having strong orientation for new staff with clear policies, rules, and specialized training that addresses the hard work they will be faced with. There must be opportunities for regular staff meetings with leadership to debrief, as well as opportunities to meet one-on-one to reflect on the stress of caring for children who are experiencing disruptive change in their lives. As the director did in the situation with the twins, here's what those in an administrative position must do:

- Be aware and embrace that when challenges surface, a solution can be found—many times collectively.

- Understand that not one person is perfect, and until a staff member or parent proves differently, everyone should be trusted and treated equally.

- Listen actively and intently—model patience and understanding.

- Provide direction by using daily written and oral communication, and be willing to be that extra set of hands should issues arise in the classroom or during exchanges with parents.

- Encourage others in leadership positions as they continue to learn how to lead and manage, while also supporting staff working in classrooms with busy children.

We covered several tools in chapter 3 that can help those in the program environment learn more about one another, and we saw how useful those tools are in the subsequent chapters. By utilizing in these tools when appropriate, everyone involved can better recognize the commitment necessary to do this work—day in and day out—especially when serving children experiencing disruptive change. Being open to gathering information on a regular basis allows everyone within the program space to gain insight on each person's perspective and facilitates informative decision making. Using this insight in tandem with the ongoing coaching and mentoring, reflective supervision and staff training (to include learning communities) creates connections by and between teaching staff.

When program staff members enjoy one another, their calm and genuine interactions influence the way children feel and benefit development and learning (Mashburn et al. 2008; Landry et al. 2014). Coaching and mentoring support individuals in a positive fashion as well as enhance their teaching practices and allow them to reflect on their daily interactions and planning for the children in their care. Staff members who make personal connections nurture relationships together, and this ultimately creates a sense of teamwork.

Reflective supervision that occurs at least weekly allows staff to see themselves more clearly by acknowledging situations and feelings that arise when working with challenging children. Trust is an important component to this process, since staff members will express uncomfortable emotions and situations. Listening and reflecting allow staff to feel heard and to problem solve situations that will continually arise.

Finally, staff need ongoing training and opportunities to participate in learning communities. Informal and formal opportunities, such as local workshops, conferences, online webinars or short courses, and classes at local universities, are all viable options. In addition, facilitated learning communities supported either within the program environment or by local early childhood professional organizations foster professional learning where the individuals in attendance share their experience and expertise. A skilled facilitator is a necessary element to support a successful learning community design (Gerdes and Jefferson 2015). Those who participate are motivated and inspired to think critically about their daily practices and hear how others are adjusting and adapting their classroom environments to better care for children. By offering a variety of options, those in early childhood positions are supported to be lifelong learners.

Nothing is more toxic than burnout. Whether working alone or in a program environment, burnout can be exhausting not only for the person experiencing it but also for coworkers and, most significalntly, the children. Caring for oneself and others means finding ways to manage stress. For example, during her directing days, Dr. Jane would often go for walks and also sought outside professional colleagues to confer with, especially when situations seemed too complicated to figure out. Kari had colleagues at her workplace who would meet once a month for a night out, and they could not talk about work—that was the one rule. The focus was on fun and fellowship. *Finding Your Smile Again* by Jeff Johnson offers these practical suggestions:

- **Have a positive outlook:** Think positively about situations and people, as this has beneficial outcomes.

- **Cultivate self-awareness:** Know who you are, which gives you power and control of your life.

- **Have a healthy amount of selfishness:** Recognize that your own needs are valid, and do what is necessary to meet them.

- **Relinquish control:** By doing this, we become a bit more flexible and better able to deal with change.

- **Have a playful attitude:** Allow yourself to explore your ideas, dreams, thoughts, and fears through a child's eyes.

- **Make thoughtful choices:** Slow down enough to make thoughtful, mindful choices while also recognizing that your choices may not always lead to the end results you wanted.

Working with challenging children is exhausting. Program leadership in group and school settings must be supportive. Those working in the family child care home environment must find connection with others. Brainstorming with others in the field creates opportunities for relationships that provide informal support systems that can also make connections to more formal supports. By accessing quality resources, you can be better informed. While not an exhaustive list, the appendix provides many online resources. Creating "heard" opportunities, where one can voice concerns, serves as the cornerstone of hope and help for children and their families, which leads to our final suggestion: access to an early childhood mental health consultant.

Several stories in our book featured Kari in her role as an early childhood mental health consultant. Communities across the nation are embracing this service support for early childhood professionals. Some individuals providing specialized service are child development specialists, behavioral health therapists, psychologists, and social workers. These outside perspectives help to support those working on the front line who must deal with children who have experienced distress and feel threatened. Their expertise helps to identify strategies and activities that help early childhood professionals reestablish a sense of safety and control. It is critical that classroom environments, large or small, be safe—they must be trauma-sensitive spaces where adults support children in creating positive self-identities. The early childhood mental health consultant can provide suggestions as well as the necessary links families must access to assist in their healing. The consultant also provides perspective and support for those teachers and caregivers who carry the weight of the work. The consultant also helps in processing the child's and family's life circumstances in a fashion that provides perspective, which is sometimes hard to remember to do based on the circumstances at hand. As noted earlier in the book, it is those "invisible bags" that are cluttering classrooms and disrupting daily activity. An early childhood mental health consultant's insight can help to check those bags at the door of the facility where they can be stored rather than take up necessary program environment space.

Unfortunately, events just like the day Dr. Jane experienced more than twenty years ago and the shifts and changes in today's society will continue and result in disruptive change in the lives of children. The world has watched over the years as the Oklahoma Standard steered groups of people to help one another by erecting a place of solitude, remembrance, hope, and education.

This spirit of generosity radiates from within the lessons learned in Oklahoma City and plays out again each time strangers come to the aid of others, as during other horrific events, both large and small, that have taken place over the years. Collectively, work has been done at many levels and in all parts of the world to create opportunity for tremendous learning about trauma and resilience. Now more than ever, strong focus is being placed on research that better informs those working in the field of early childhood.

All of the situations shared in this book were facilitated by early childhood professionals who were committed to helping children and their families have a fighting chance and experience the opportunity to find a successful trajectory.

These children and the thousands of other children like them need early childhood programs and professionals who embrace a collective vision of hope to serve as their bedrock. Take the perspective of Nobel Prize–winner Mother Teresa. When asked, "It must be dreadful working with these sick children and then so many die anyway. How can you stand their dying?" she is reported to have answered, "We love them while they're here." She reflected a total commitment to what she was doing *in the moment* rather than worrying about the future or sorrow of those lost. This type of detached concern didn't reduce her interest in what she was doing; rather, this expression of personal power was characterized by *more* commitment. We hope that by reading our book, you have become empowered and further committed to serve those children and their families who must have unconditional love, support, and encouragement to navigate the disruptive change in their lives.

Appendix

Classroom Resources

Fiddle Focus® for Busy Hands

Use this tool to offer a unique sensory experience. The variety of fabrics provides a diversity of touch and textures. It also has a loop feature that's ideal for attaching additional focus items, such as visual schedules or other learning-oriented products. You can find this item at www.cessllc.org.

Fiddle Focus® for Busy Fingers

This is a multicolor fabric texture product perfect for mounting on any location where children need to sit and focus. This can include a desk, table, or other areas where fingers can be busy while focusing on a task. The interior of the product is a durable rubber that provides a "push" sensation in addition to the multiple fabric textures. These items can be washed in cold water and remounted to the same location using the provided Velcro strip. They can be found at www.cessllc.org.

Mad Jar

Take a plastic container and cover with labels you make on the computer. Label suggestions include the following words: *mad*, *angry*, *frustrated*, *disappointed*, *scared*, and *shouting*. These labels can be affixed using a glue stick and then covered in clear contact paper for durability. The Mad Jar can then be placed in various locations in the classroom or in an individual child's cubby, or it can be offered as a suggestion for home use.

Visual Schedules

A First/Then schedule with pages for what happens first, second, third, fourth, and fifth along with coordinating picture cards of actions that children must generally do in a group or home environment allows a child to visually see what is happening next. For example, "First I will eat lunch" (picture is of children and adults eating); "Then I will go outside" (picture is of children playing on a playground). The use of these visual schedules along with the picture cards assist adults in communicating with children who need to "see" the process.

Get It Back Together Bag

Using a simple gift bag, include four smaller containers with quick physical activity choices for children to pull from the bag when they are struggling. Simply offering the bag and asking children to choose gets their attention and then allows the adult to process through the choice. If it's "hop five times" or "blow out your birthday candles," the adult can do the activity with the child or simply use it as an opportunity to help the child regain composure. Adding more activity ideas is certainly encouraged, and customizing for a certain child is suggested.

Pool Noodle Squish

Cut six- to twelve-inch sections from a pool noodle. Some children benefit from squeezing or even biting something when they are stressed (adult supervision is advised). Some children like to carry around the foam piece or need to hang on to it when sitting in story time.

Defined Sitting Spaces

Many children need a defined space and a little "cush and rolling" feeling to participate in story time, lunch, or any other activities when sitting is necessary. Provide beach balls, blow-up bathtub headrests, and textured place mats for this purpose. Partially filling a beach ball with air provides an instant option.

Sensory Boxes or Baskets

Having a variety of items to touch and squeeze is relaxing to children because of their being able to manipulate these objects. A variety of soft, textured items, such as the Fiddle Focus for Busy Hands, can be combined in boxes or baskets and available to all children when they need them.

Pinwheels

Research has shown time and time again that nice deep breaths calm all of us down! Allowing a child to hold and focus on a colorful spinning pinwheel will engage her while an adult talks her through a frustrating moment.

Organizational Resources

Blueprint for Action, Third Edition, by Paula Jorde Bloom

Blueprint for Action is designed as a practical resource for early childhood program leaders who are serious about improving the quality of their programs from the lens of organizational systems and their interactions. Assessment tools are provided in the book and are available on a CD-ROM from the publisher, New Horizons (www.newhorizonsbooks.net). This is where access to the *Early Childhood Work Environment Survey* (ECWES) can also be found. The assessment tools may be reproduced for professional development purposes at your early childhood program.

- *Preschool Teaching Practices* (Assessment Tool #12) focuses on assessing teaching practices in the preschool classroom.

- *Infant-Toddler Teaching Practices* (Assessment Tool #13) focuses on assessing teaching practices in the infant-toddler classroom.

- *Communication Style* (Assessment Tool #17) obtains a greater understanding by and between all staff within a program's space for how each person sends, receives, and interprets communication.

- *Learning Style* (Assessment Tool #14) provides an awareness of each person's learning style to best assist individuals with their learning.

Early Childhood Environment Rating Scales

Directors and leaders can use these scales to assess process quality in an early childhood setting. The scales assess interactions between staff and children, parents, and other adults; interactions between staff members; and the interactions children have with the many materials and activities in the environment.

- *ECERS-R The Early Childhood Environment Rating Scale* by Thelma Harms, Richard M. Clifford, and Debby Cryer

- *ITERS-R The Infant/Toddler Environment Rating Scale* by Thelma Harms, Debby Cryer, and Richard M. Clifford

- *FCCERS-R The Family Child Care Environment Rating Scale* by Thelma Harms, Debby Cryer, and Richard M. Clifford

***The Visionary Director: A Handbook for Dreaming, Organizing, and Improvising in Your Center*, Second Edition, by Margie Carter and Deb Curtis**

This book offers a framework for thinking about and organizing the work as an early childhood program leader. Within the text, find principles and strategies to cultivate the kind of thinking and activities that support a vision of early childhood programs as learning communities based on a conceptual framework.

Recommended Websites

Administration for Children and Families www.acf.hhs.gov

Administration on Intellectual and Development Disabilities www.acl.gov
/programs/aidd/index.aspx

Alcoholics Anonymous www.aa.org

Alexander Graham Bell Association for the Deaf and Hard of Hearing
www.agbell.org

Allergy & Asthma Network www.allergyasthmanetwork.org

American Academy of Child & Adolescent Psychiatry www.aacap.org

American Academy of Pediatrics www.aap.org

American Association of Kidney Patients www.aakp.org

American Cancer Society www.cancer.org/treatment/childrenandcancer/
helpingchildrenwhenafamilymemberhascancer/index

American Diabetes Association www.diabetes.org

American SIDS Institute http://sids.org

Autism Speaks www.autismspeaks.org

Center for Parent Information and Resources www.parentcenterhub.org

Center on the Developing Child at Harvard University http://developingchild
.harvard.edu

Center on the Social and Emotional Foundations for Learning http://csefel
.vanderbilt.edu

Centers for Disease Control and Prevention www.cdc.gov

Child Care Aware http://childcareaware.org

Child Development Institute http://childdevelopmentinfo.com

Child Molestation Research & Prevention Institute www.childmolestation
prevention.org

Child Welfare Information Gateway www.childwelfare.gov

Child Welfare League of America www.cwla.org

Childhelp www.childhelp.org

Children and Adults with Attention-Deficit/Hyperactivity Disorder
www.chadd.org

Children's Defense Fund www.childrensdefense.org

Coalition to Stop Gun Violence http://csgv.org

Council for Exceptional Children www.cec.sped.org

Department of Homeland Security www.dhs.gov

Early Childhood Training and Technical Assistance System www.acf.hhs.gov
/ecd/interagency-projects/ece-technical-assistance

Epilepsy Foundation www.epilepsy.com

Federal Emergency Management Agency www.fema.gov

Genetic Alliance www.geneticalliance.org

HealthCare coverage www.healthcare.gov

Healthy Child Care America www.healthychildcare.org

Military OneSource www.militaryonesource.mil

National Association for the Education of Young Children www.naeyc.org

National Association for Family Child Care www.nafcc.org

National Center for Children in Poverty www.nccp.org

National Center for PTSD www.ptsd.va.gov

National Center on Family Homelessness www.familyhomelessness.org

National Center on Shaken Baby Syndrome http://dontshake.org

National Child Traumatic Stress Network www.nctsn.org

National Children's Advocacy Center www.nationalcac.org

National Coalition for the Homeless http://nationalhomeless.org

National Crime Prevention Council www.ncpc.org

National Down Syndrome Society www.ndss.org

National Fatherhood Initiative www.fatherhood.org

National Foster Care Month www.childwelfare.gov/fostercaremonth

National Hospice and Palliative Care Organization www.nhpco.org

National Institute of Mental Health www.nimh.nih.gov/index.shtml

National Parent Helpline www.nationalparenthelpline.org

National Sexual Violence Resource Center www.nsvrc.org

National Stepfamily Resource Center www.stepfamilies.info

National Technical Assistance Center for Children's Mental Health http://
gucchdtacenter.georgetown.edu

National Weather Service www.weather.gov/owlie

Parent Advocacy Coalition for Educational Rights (PACER) Center www.pacer.org

Parents Without Partners www.parentswithoutpartners.org

Prevent Child Abuse America www.preventchildabuse.org

Resources Especially for Foster or Adoptive Families www.parentcenterhub.org /repository/fosteradoptive

Sesame Street www.sesamestreet.org

STAR Institute for Sensory Processing Disorder www.spdstar.org

Stop It Now! (Prevent Sexual Abuse) www.stopitnow.org

Substance Abuse and Mental Health Services Administration www.samhsa.gov

Technical Assistance Center on Social Emotional Intervention http://challenging behavior.fmhi.usf.edu/index.htm

The Early Childhood Technical Assistance Center http://ectacenter.org

The Fred Rogers Company www.fredrogers.org/parents

The National Domestic Violence Hotline www.thehotline.org

Tribal Early Childhood Research Center www.ucdenver.edu/academics /colleges/PublicHealth/research/centers/CAIANH/trc/Pages/TRC.aspx

US Department of Education www.ed.gov

Zero to Three http://www.zerotothree.org

Recommended Children's Books

Changing Parental Relationships

And Tango Makes Three by J. Richardson and P. Parnell (2005): A story about two male penguins at the Central Park Zoo raising their baby.

Bessie Bump Gets a New Family by A. Meredith and N. Lee (2010): A turtle child copes with the separation and divorce of her parents.

Daddy, Papa, and Me by L. Newman (2009): Families come in all shapes, colors, genders, and sizes. These two fathers adopted a little boy and gave him a wonderful family.

A Day with Dad by B. Holmberg (2008): Shows how the love between a child and an estranged parent can remain strong regardless of how far apart they are.

Dinosaurs Divorce by Laurie Krasny Brown and Marc Brown (1988): Helps young children between the ages of three and seven deal with the trauma of divorce.

Heather Has Two Mommies by L. Newman (2015): An adopted little girl named Heather has a wonderful life with her two mommies.

I Am Living in 2 Homes by Garcelle Beauvais and Sebastian A. Jones (2014): A story of two children dealing with the divorce of their parents.

I Don't Want to Talk about It by J. Ransom and K. Finney (2000): A story of how two parents help their child get through and understand divorce.

It Wasn't My Fault by H. Lester (1985): A story that deals with blame as well as taking responsibility for yourself.

It's Not Your Fault, Koko Bear by V. Lansky (1997): Helps to teach children that it's not their fault their parents divorced, and that although their parents are divorced, they still love them.

Let's Talk about It: Divorce by F. Rogers (1996): A book about divorce, and how families and children can deal with it.

Mommy, Mama, and Me by L. Newman (2009). A story about two mommies who care for their adopted daughter as a family.

Mum and Dad Glue by K. Gray (2009): Acknowledges the emotional challenges children may feel when parents divorce or separate.

My Bonus Mom! Taking the Step out of Stepmom by Tami Butcher (2011): Helps children understand divorce and the addition of new stepparents.

My Family's Changing by P. Thomas (1999): Helps young children ages four through eight deal with separation from a parent.

My Mother's Getting Married by J. Drescher (1986): How a young girl deals with her mother getting remarried.

My Mother's House, My Father's House by C. B. Christiansen (1989): A child describes having two different houses in which to live—"my mother's house" and "my father's house"—and what it is like to travel back and forth between them.

Room for Rabbit by R. Schotter (2003): A child's story about adjusting to living between Mom's house and Dad and Stepmom's house.

Standing on My Own Two Feet: A Child's Affirmation of Love in the Midst of Divorce by T. Schmitz (2008): A child's story of dealing with his parents' divorce.

Two Homes by C. Masurel (2001): Explains the benefits of living in two different homes and that the child is loved just as much as before the divorce.

Was It the Chocolate Pudding? A Story for Little Kids about Divorce by S. Levins (2005): A young child's perspective when parents announce they are getting a divorce.

Weekends with Dad: What to Expect When Your Parents Divorce by M. Higgins (2011): Tells how a child will not see Dad every day, but every weekend.

What Can I Do? A Book for Children of Divorce by D. Lowry and B. Matthews (2001): Expresses the emotions that a young girl went through when her parents told her they were divorcing.

Why Don't I Have a Daddy? by G. A. Clay (2008): Presents the basic facts of anonymous donor conception in a simple but loving manner.

Community Violence

Smoky Night by E. Bunting (1994): A child's view of urban violence when a young boy and his mother are forced to flee their apartment during a night of rioting in Los Angeles.

Stan the Timid Turtle by L. Fox (2014): A story about a turtle who is trying to cope with his fears and school violence.

Why Did It Happen? Helping Children Cope in a Violent World by J. Cohn (1994): A story concerning the robbery of a neighborhood grocery store and how one boy comes to terms with the event.

Domestic Violence and Abuse

Because It's My Body! by Joanne Sherman (2006): Focused on empowerment and preventions, this book gives young children a way to reject unwanted and possibly harmful contact by adults and other children.

The Day My Daddy Lost His Temper by Carol Santana McCleary (2014): Use this book to help children verbalize their feelings and experiences to assist with the healing process of witnessing and living within a home with domestic abuse.

A Family That Fights by Sharon Chesler Bernstein (1991): Deals with family fighting and domestic violence.

Hands Are Not for Hitting by Martine Agassi (2002): Helps children learn that violence is never okay.

Hear My Roar: A Story of Family Violence by Gillian Watts (2009): A mother and her bear cub seek support from Dr. Owl because of the father's yelling.

I Can't Talk about It: A Child's Book about Sexual Abuse by Doris Sanford (1986): A child reveals her father's sexual abuse to a dove that helps her heal and learn to trust again.

I Said No! A Kid-to-Kid Guide to Keeping Private Parts Private by Zack and Kimberly King (2010): Written from a child's point of view, *I Said No!* helps children set healthy boundaries for their private parts and describes how to deal with inappropriate behavior by others.

Mommy's Black Eye by William George Bentrim (2009): Helps explain the very complicated issue of domestic violence to young children.

One of the Problems of Everett Anderson by Lucille Clifton (2001): A child wonders how he can help his friend who appears to be a victim of child abuse.

Please Tell! A Child's Story about Sexual Abuse by Jessie (1991): A child who was sexually molested by a family member reaches out to give other children courage to tell.

A Safe Place by Maxine Trottier (1997): A young girl and her mother live in a shelter to escape from an abusive loved one.

Something Is Wrong at My House: A Book about Parents' Fighting, revised edition by Diane Davis (2010): Helps children understand and cope when their parents fight.

Stop Picking on Me: A First Look at Bullying by Pat Thomas (2000): Explores the difficult issue of bullying in reassuringly simple terms.

When Mommy Got Hurt: A Story for Young Children about Domestic Violence by Ilene Lee and Kathy Sylwester (2011): Mom is a victim of domestic violence and takes her child to live with Grandma.

The Words Hurt: Helping Children Cope with Verbal Abuse by Chris Loftis (2006): A story about a boy and the verbal abuse he suffers from his father.

Foster Care and Adoption

Families Change: A Book for Children Experiencing Termination of Parental Rights by J. Nelson (2007): A story about children being able to understand why they had to change their living situation and why it's not their fault.

Foster Families by S. L. Schuette (2010): With use of simple text and photographs, this book presents how foster families interact with one another.

How I Was Adopted by J. Cole (1999): The story of how one child was adopted.

I Don't Have Your Eyes by C. Kitze (2003): For transracial and transcultural adoptees and domestic adoptees, and for children in foster care or kinship placements. This book celebrates the differences within their families as well as the similarities that connect them.

I Wished for You: An Adoption Story by M. Richmond (2008): Explains to children how much their parents loved them and the adoption process.

Kids Need to Be Safe: A Book for Children in Foster Care by J. Nelson (2005): A book about how children are important and how sometimes they must live in foster homes to be safe.

Maybe Days: A Book for Children in Foster Care by J. Wilgocki and M. K. Wright (2002): Helps young children ages four and up who are going into or have just gone into foster care.

Murphy's Three Homes: A Story for Children in Foster Care by J. Gilman Levinson (2008): A boy moves from one house to another and begins to understand all his sad and angry feelings and finds ways to cope. Eventually, he finds a comfortable spot in a new home.

Our Twitchey by K. Gray and M. McQuillan (2003): A young bunny realizes he is different from his parents. He finds out that his parents are actually his adoptive parents and that they love him unconditionally.

Over the Moon: An Adoption Tale by K. Katz (1997): A story about international adoption.

Spark Learns to Fly by J. Foxon (2007): A story about violence in the home that results in a child having to go into foster care.

The Star by C. Miller Lovell (2005): A story about a child learning to cope with living in foster care.

Tell Me Again about the Night I Was Born by J. L. Curtis (2000): A story about a child who was adopted by parents the night she was born.

We Belong Together by T. Parr (2007): How families come together through adoption.

Grief and Loss from Death or Changing Family Situations

After Charlotte's Mom Died by C. Spelman (1996): Charlotte and her father struggle with the death of her mother and undergo therapy to share their feelings and build their new relationship.

Always and Forever by A. Durant and D. Gliori (2004): A family of forest animals learns to cope with the death of a loved one.

Baby Sister by D. M. Sachs (1986): The story of a little boy who is adjusting to the birth of his sister after many years as an only child.

Badger's Parting Gifts by S. Varley (1992): Helps young children ages four through eight deal with the death of a loved one.

Bear's Last Journey by U. Weigelt (2003): A picture book illustrating the sense of loss and confusion children may feel when a loved one dies.

Boomer's Big Day by C. McGeorge (1994): Waiting for his daily walk, Boomer realizes that it isn't any ordinary day—his family is moving.

Christmas Moon by D. Cazet (1984): The story of a young boy who misses his grandfather during the holiday season, and how he remembers him and all the fun things they did together.

Clover's Secret by C. M. Winn and D. Walsh (1996): In an imaginary land where people can fly, two girls form a friendship that helps one of them deal with the problems she faces at home.

Dog Heaven by C. Rylant (1995): Depicts a happy place for all dogs, where they can enjoy the things they loved most.

Everett Anderson's Goodbye by L. Clifton (1983): The story of a young boy throughout the stages of grief coping with the death of his father.

Feelings to Share from A to Z by T. Snow, P. Snow, and C. Hartman (2007): Preschoolers often do not know how to express the way they feel. This book introduces children to emotional vocabulary words in order to help them express themselves.

Geranium Morning by E. S. Powell (1990): Two friends who lose parents, one suddenly in an accident and one by illness, learn to deal with their grief.

Goodbye House by Frank Asch (1989): Assists children in understanding the process of moving and the excitement of a new place.

Goodbye Mousie by R. Harris (2001): A story about the loss of a beloved pet.

The Good-Bye Book by J. Viorst (1988): A child, on the verge of being left behind by parents who are going out for the evening, comes up with a variety of pleas and excuses.

Good-bye Jeepers by N. Loewen (2012): Helps children deal with the loss of a pet that has died.

Grandma and Grandpa's Garden by N. Griffiths (2007): A story about the death of a grandparent and dealing with grief.

I Like Where I Am by J. Harper (2004): An up-tempo story about a boy who has experienced a recent move and is sad.

A Little Bit of Rob by B. J. Turner (1995): A story of a young girl whose brother has died, and how she and her family find ways to cope and move forward together.

I Miss You: A First Look at Death by P. Thomas and L. Harker (2001): Helps children understand that death is a natural complement to life.

I Miss You! A Military Kid's Book about Deployment by Beth Andrews (2007): Explains what a child may feel during a deployment and how to express those feelings.

I Wish I Had My Father by N. Simon (1983): How Father's Day is tough for a boy whose father left him years ago and never communicates with him.

I'm Not Moving, Mama! by Nancy White Carlstrom (1999): A story about moving to a new place to live and change.

The Invisible String by P. Karst and G. Stevenson (2000): Teaches the importance of attachment and love to each other.

Jamaica's Blue Marker by J. Havill (2003): Helps young children ages four through seven deal with the trauma of moving.

Jim's Dog Muffins by M. Cohen (1986): Jim's friend at school helps him overcome his sadness at the death of his pet dog.

Lifetimes: The Beautiful Way to Explain Death to Children by B. Mellonie and R. Ingpen (1983): Introduces children to death with pictures, animals, and flowers, in a way that is not frightening or scary.

Llama Llama Misses Mama by A. Dewdney (2009): A book that focuses on being left the first day of school.

Missing Mommy by R. Cobb (2013): A story of a boy, told from his point of view, who doesn't understand his mother's death, and how learns how to cope with it.

My Sister Is an Alien by Rachel Bright (2010): Helps young ones adjust to having a new baby (brother or sister) in the house.

Nana Upstairs and Nana Downstairs by T. dePaola (2000): A young boy deals with the death of his nana.

No Matter What by D. Gliori (2008): A book explaining the loss of a loved one.

Remembering Crystal by S. Loth (2010): The story of the loss of a friend and how a true friendship is a gift that doesn't die.

Rudi's Pond by Eve Bunting (2004): Children try to understand the loss of a classmate and remember him by building a pond.

Sally Goes to Heaven by S. Huneck (2014): A beloved dog dies and goes to heaven, where she lives happily and finds her family on earth a new pet.

Samantha Jane's Missing Smile by J. Kaplow and D. Pincus (2007): A story about a young girl learning to cope with the loss of a parent.

Sammy in the Sky by Barbara Walsh (2011): A story that helps children understand the death of a pet.

Saying Goodbye to Your Pet by M. Heegaard (2001): Helps children cope with the loss of a pet through drawing.

The Scar by C. Moundlic (2011): Helps young children deal with a death of a parent.

Sometimes We Were Brave by Pat Brisson (2010): The story of a child who misses his mother, who is deployed.

Stones for Grandpa by R. Londner and J. M. Avilés (2013): A little boy and his family gather at the cemetery for the unveiling of his beloved grandpa's gravestone, and bring stones to place on the grave, as is the Jewish tradition.

Tear Soup: A Recipe for Healing after Loss by P. Schwiebert and C. DeKlyen (1999): Processing grief after a loved one dies.

Waiting to Sing by H. Kaplan (2000): How a young boy deals with the death of his mother.

Water Bugs and Dragonflies: Explaining Death to Young Children by D. Stickney (2009): Using a metaphor of water bugs changing into dragonflies, this book explains what happens when someone passes away.

When My Mommy and Daddy Leave Me at Daycare by C. Couchois (2014): Teaches children how to deal with separation anxiety.

Whimsy's Heavy Things by J. Kraulis (2013): A story about changing the things that weighs us down into the things that lift us up.

You Hold Me and I'll Hold You by J. Carson (1992): When a great-aunt dies, a young child finds comfort in being held and in holding too.

Homelessness

Along Came a Dog by M. DeJong (1980): A story of two homeless animals that meet and eventually become friends and protect each other.

Esperanza Rising by P. M. Ryan (2002): A young girl and her mother escape depression in their country but are then faced with being homeless.

The Family under the Bridge by N. S. Carlson (1989): The story of a man who adopted a family of children who lived under a bridge.

Fly Away Home by E. Bunting and R. Himler (1991): The story of a homeless boy and his dad who are hiding in an airport; a trapped bird that becomes free gives them inspiration.

Mutt Dog! by S. M. King (2005): A story of a homeless dog that is seeking a home.

A Shelter in Our Car by M. Gunning (2013): A child and her mom's experiences of being homeless after immigrating to the United States.

Incarceration

My Daddy Is in Jail by J. Bender (2003): A child learns about living apart from a dad who is in jail.

The Night Dad Went to Jail by M. Higgins (2013): Helps young children ages four through eight deal with having an incarcerated parent.

Visiting Day by J. Woodson and J. E. Ransome (2015): The story of a young girl and her grandmother's monthly preparations to visit her incarcerated father.

What Is Jail, Mommy? by J. Stranglin (2006): The story of a mother telling her child that her father is going to jail.

Natural and Human-Made Disasters

The Ant Hill Disaster by J. Cook (2014): Helps young children ages five through eight deal with natural and human-made disasters.

Earthquake! by M. Bauer (2009): Discovers and explains what creates an earthquake and how to stay safe.

Hurricane by J. London (1998): A young boy describes his family's experiences when a hurricane hits their home on the island of Puerto Rico.

I Survived True Stories: Five Epic Disasters by L. Tarshis (2014): For older children, this book provides true stories of how children survived disasters and lived to tell their stories of survival that seem unimaginable.

Jenny Is Scared: When Sad Things Happen in the World by C. Shuman and C. Pillo (2003): A comforting coping story for children who are aware of the threats of violence and terrorism in the world. A range of fears, feelings, and questions are explored, and the child reader is encouraged to talk to parents, friends, and other caregivers.

Lorelita the Hurricane Hound by E. Antinis (2014): The effects of a hurricane told through a dog's point of view.

We Have Tornadoes: Tell Me Why by L. Brennan (2014): Why, how, and what to do during a tornado.

Special Need or Medical Illness (Children and Adults)

Autism: Living with My Brother Tiger by L. Lee (2006): An eight-year-old boy's life is disrupted by the birth of a sibling severely affected by autism, including his day-to-day struggles and changes to the life he once knew.

David and the Worry Beast: Helping Children Cope with Anxiety by A. M. Guanci (2007): Addresses a child's anxiety and ways to cope with his "worry beast."

Dealing with Feeling Sad by I. Thomas (2013): Describes for children what sadness is and ways to deal with it.

Don't Panic, Annika by J. C. Bell (2011): A child panics at almost everything that causes her problems. She learns how to stay calm and think through the problem with guidance from her family.

An Elephant in the Living Room by J. M. Hastings and M. H. Typpo (1984): A child lives with a parent who has substance abuse addictions.

Franklin Goes to the Hospital by P. Bourgeois (2011): Franklin turtle puts on a brave face when going to the hospital.

The Great Katie Kate by M. Deland (2010): Provides a way for parents and medical professionals to help children understand their condition in a positive way and to overcome their fears.

Grump Groan Growl by B. Hooks and C. Raschka (2008): A book about emotions that gives children permission to experience how they feel. Can be used with any situation.

Happy Pants: Why Is Mummy So Sad? by H. Gallagher (2014): Explains to a child mom's postpartum depression after the new baby comes home.

Leah's Voice by L. DeMonia (2012): Sisters demonstrate how they relate to one another, even though one has autism.

Little Tree: A Story for Children with Serious Medical Problems by J. C. Mills (2003): A story of resilience when faced with serious medical problems.

Mommy Stayed in Bed This Morning: Helping Children Understand Depression by M. Weaver (2002): Helps preschool-age children understand depression as a mental illness, as told through a child's point of view.

Mummy's Lump by G. Forrest (2015): Helps a child understand mom's cancer and illness.

My Brother Charlie by H. Peete-Robinson and R. E. Peete (2010): Told from a big sister's perspective, this story is about a brother who happens to be autistic.

My Brother Is Autistic by J. Mallinos-Moore (2008): Investigates a sibling's feelings about having a brother with autism.

Nana's Helping Hand with PTSD by A. Miranda (2015): Helps children learn more about PTSD.

Please Don't Cry, Mom by H. Denboer (1994): A child learns how to cope with his mother's depression.

The Purple Balloon by C. Rascka (2007): The story of a boy who is aware of his pending death and is able to express the way he feels.

Ringo the Flamingo by N. Griffiths (2015): A story that challenges preconceptions about disabilities.

Sad Days, Glad Days: A Story about Depression by D. Hamilton (1995): A young girl tries to understand her mother's depression, which sometimes leads to her sleeping all day, feeling sad, or crying.

Silly Billy by A. Browne (2007): Billy worries a lot. In this story he takes a trip to his grandmother's and learns how to overcome some of his fears.

Someone I Love Died by Suicide by D. T. Cammarata (2009): A child loses someone through suicide.

Someone I Love Is Sick: Helping Very Young Children Cope with Cancer in the Family by K. McCue (2009): Addresses the stages of cancer and explains it to children.

Sometimes by R. Elliott (2011): Little brother and big sister deal with a disability that sends her to the hospital.

Sometimes My Mommy Gets Angry by B. M. Campbell (2005): A story of a girl living with her mentally ill mother.

Talking Is Hard for Me! by L. Reinert (2013): Helps children with speech delays deal with the frustrations this sometimes causes.

A Terrible Thing Happened by M. M. Holmes, S. J. Mudlaff, and C. Pillo (2000): After a traumatic incident, a child becomes anxious and then angry until a counselor helps him talk about these emotions to help him feel better.

This Much I Know by H. Barnard (2015): A young girl learns to cope with her mother having breast cancer.

We'll Paint the Octopus Red by S. Bodeen-Stuve (1998): A six-year-old girl is very excited to welcome her new sibling, who is diagnosed with Down syndrome, into the world.

Wemberly Worried by K. Henkes (2011): A mouse worries too much about everything.

What about Me? by W. Bentrim (2010): A child feels abandoned because a sibling is very ill.

What about Me? When Brothers and Sisters Get Sick by A. Peterkin (1992): This story, narrated by a sibling of a sick child, goes through many of the questions and concerns that a child might be thinking and feeling when a sibling is sick.

When My Mommy Cries by C. LaPoint (2012): A little girl discovers the safety and security of her mother's love, even though depression and sadness is a part of their lives.

When Will I Feel Better? Understanding Chronic Illness by R. P. Monroe (1998): Helps children work through understanding the difficult issue of dealing with illness.

Why Am I So Tired? A First Look at . . . Diabetes by P. Thomas (2008): A story explaining diabetes to a child who has been diagnosed.

Why Are You So Sad? A Child's Book about Parental Depression by B. Andrews and N. Wong (2002): A child has a mom who often seems cranky and is suffering from depression.

Why, Charlie Brown, Why? A Story about What Happens When a Friend Is Very Ill by C. Schultz (2002): A story of how children are dealing with their friend's cancer diagnosis.

Why Jimmy Can't Sit Still by S. Tunis (2004): Shares the struggles of a child with ADHD and tells what fellow students may witness.

References

Ainsworth, M.D., M. Blehar, E. Waters, and S. Wall. 1978. *Patterns of Attachment*. Hillsdale, NJ: Erlbaum.

Bloom, P. 2015. *Blueprint for Action: Leading Your Team in Continuous Quality Improvement*, 3rd ed. Lake Forest, IL: New Horizons.

Bowlby, John. 1969. *Attachment and Loss: Vol. 1. Attachment*. New York: Basic Books.

Carter, M., and D. Curtis. 2008. *Learning Together with Young Children*. St. Paul, MN: Redleaf Press.

———. 2010. *The Visionary Director: A Handbook for Dreaming, Organizing, and Improvising in Your Center*. St. Paul, MN: Redleaf Press.

Center on the Developing Child at Harvard University. 2011. "Building the Brain's 'Air Traffic Control' System: How Early Experiences Shape the Development of Executive Function: Working Paper No. 11." www.developingchild.harvard.edu.

Child Welfare Information Gateway. 2014. "Foster Care Statistics 2014." www.childwelfare.gov/pubPDFs/foster.pdf.

Diamond, A., and K. Lee. 2011. "Interventions Shown to Aid Executive Function Development in Children 4 to 12 Years Old." *Science* 333:959–64.

Dombro, Amy Laura, Judy R. Jablon, and Charlotte Stetson. 2011. *Powerful Interactions: How to Connect with Children to Extend Their Learning*. Washington, DC: National Association for the Education of Young Children.

Donahue, P., B. Falk, and A. Provet. 2000. *Mental Health Consultation in Early Childhood*. Baltimore, MD: Brookes Publishing.

Dunn, W. 1997. "The Impact of Sensory Processing Abilities on the Daily Lives of Young Children and Their Families: A Conceptual Model." *Infants and Young Children* 9 (4): 23–35.

Eggbeer, L., T. Mann, and N. Siebel. 2007. "Reflective Supervision: Past, Present, and Future." *Zero to Three* 28 (2): 5–9.

Epstein, A. 2007. *The Intentional Teacher: Choosing the Best Strategies for Young Children's Learning.* Washington, DC: National Association for the Education of Young Children.

Felitti, V. J., R. F. Anda, D. Nordenberg, D. F. Williamson, A. M. Spitz, V. Edwards, M. P. Koss, and J. S. Marks. 1998. "The Relationship of Adult Health Status to Childhood Abuse and Household Dysfunction." *American Journal of Preventative Medicine* 14:245–58.

Galinsky, E. 2010. *Mind in the Making.* New York: HarperCollins.

Gerdes, J., and T. Jefferson. 2015. "How a Professional Learning Community Changed a Family Child Care Provider's Beliefs and Practices." *Young Children* 70 (5): 8–13.

Gilkerson, L., and R. Shahmoon-Shanok. 2000. "Relationships for Growth: Cultivating Reflective Practice in Infant, Toddler, and Preschool Programs." *In WAIMH Handbook of Infant Mental Health, Vol. 2: Early Intervention, Evaluation, and Assessment,* edited by J. D. Osofsky, and H. E. Fitzgerald, 33–79. New York: John Wiley & Sons.

Ginsburg, K., and M. Jablow. 2015. *Building Resilience in Children and Teens: Giving Kids Roots and Wings,* 3rd. ed. Elk Grove Village, IL: American Academy of Pediatrics.

Greenman, J. 2007. *Caring Spaces, Learning Places: Children's Environments That Work.* Redmond, WA: Exchange Press.

Harper Browne, C. 2014. *The Strengthening Families Approach and Protective Factors Framework: Branching Out and Reaching Deeper.* Washington, DC: Center for the Study of Social Policy.

Hemmeter, M. L. 2007. "We Are All in This Together: Supporting Children's Social Emotional Development and Addressing Challenging Behavior." *Child Care Exchange* (July/August): 12–16.

Howell, J., and K. Reinhard. 2015. *Rituals and Traditions: Fostering a Sense of Community in Preschool.* Washington, DC: National Association for the Education of Young Children.

Humphries, J., and K. Rains. 2012. "Creating In-Sync Environments for Children with Sensory Issues." *Child Care Exchange* (November/December): 53–56.

———. 2015. "Lean on Me: Helping Children and Families through Disruptive Change." *Child Care Exchange* (May/June): 87–89.

Jablon, J., A. Dombro, and S. Johnsen. 2014. *Coaching with Powerful Interactions: A Guide for Partnering with Early Childhood Teachers.* Washington, DC: National Association for the Education of Young Children.

Johnson, J. 2007. *Finding Your Smile Again: A Child Care Professional's Guide to Reducing Stress and Avoiding Burnout.* St. Paul, MN: Redleaf Press.

Kaiser, B., and J. Rasminsky. 2012. *Challenging Behavior in Young Children: Understanding, Preventing, and Responding Effectively*, 3rd ed. Upper Saddle River, NJ: Pearson.

Landry, S., T. Zucker, H. Taylor, P. Swank, J. Williams, M. Assel, A. Crawford, W. Huang, J. Clancy-Menchetti, C. Lonigan, B. Phillips, N. Eisenberg, T. Spinrad, J. deVilliers, P. deVilliers, M. Barnes, P. Starkey, and A. Klein. 2014. "Enhancing Early Child Care Quality and Learning for Toddlers at Risk: The Responsive Early Childhood Program." *Developmental Psychology* 50 (2): 526–41.

Mashburn, A., R. Pianta, B. Hamre, J. Downer, O. Barbarin, D. Bryant, M. Burchinal, R. Clifford, D. Early, and C. Howes. 2008. "Measures of Classroom Quality in Prekindergarten and Children's Development of Academic, Language, and Social Skills." *Child Development* 79 (3): 732–49.

Merriam, S., R. Caffarella, and L. Baumgartner. 1999. *Learning in Adulthood: A Comprehensive Guide.* San Francisco: Jossey-Bass.

Miyake, A., N. P. Friedman, M. J. Emerson, A. H. Witzki, A. Howerter, and T. D. Wager. 2000. "The Unity and Diversity of Executive Functions and Their Contributions to Complex 'Frontal Lobe' Tasks: A Latent Variable Analysis." *Cognitive Psychology* 41:49–100.

Moffitt, T. E., L. Arseneault, D. Belsky, N. Dickson, R. J. Hancox, H. Harrington, and A. Caspi. 2011. "A Gradient of Childhood Self-Control Predicts Health, Wealth, and Public Safety." *Proceedings of the National Academy of Sciences of the USA* 108: 2693–98.

Moore, K. A., and A. Ramirez. 2015. "Adverse Childhood Experiences and Adolescent Well-Being: Do Protective Factors Matter?" Washington, DC: *Child Trends.*

NCTSN (National Child Traumatic Stress Network). 2016. "Definition of STS." Accessed August 2, 2016. www.nctsn.org/resources/topics/secondary -traumatic-stress.

National Scientific Council on the Developing Child. 2014. "Excessive Stress Disrupts the Architecture of the Developing Brain: Working Paper 3." Updated ed. http://www.developingchild.harvard.edu.

Ostovar, R. 2009. *The Ultimate Guide to Sensory Processing Disorder: Easy, Everyday Solutions to Sensory Challenges.* Arlington, TX: Sensory World.

Perry, B. 2013. *BRIEF: Reflections on Childhood, Trauma and Society.* Houston, TX: The Child Trauma Academy Press.

Perry, D. F., M. D. Allen, E. Brennan, and J. Bradley. 2010. "The Evidence Base for Early Childhood Mental Health Consultation in Early Childhood Settings: A Research Synthesis Addressing Children's Behavioral Outcomes." *Early Education and Development* 21:795–824.

Sacks, V., D. Murphey, and K. Moore. 2014. "Adverse Childhood Experiences: National and State-Level Prevalence." *Child Trends Research Brief.* www.childtrends.org/wp-content/uploads/2014/07/Brief-adverse-childhood-experiences_FINAL.pdf.

Schiller, P. 2009. "Program Practices That Support Intentionality in Teaching." *Child Care Exchange* (January/February): 57–60.

Shonkoff, J. P., and D. A. Phillips. 2000. *From Neurons to Neighborhoods: The Science of Early Child Development.* Washington, DC: National Academy Press.

Thatcher, R. W., G. R. Lyon, J. Rumsey, and J. Krasnegor. 1996. *Developmental Neuroimaging.* San Diego, CA: Academic Press.

Zysk, V., and E. Notbohm, E. 2010. *1001 Great Ideas for Teaching and Raising Children with Autism or Asperger's.* Arlington, TX: Future Horizons.

Index